Praise for
Coachability:
The Leadership Superpower

An enormous number of books and articles have been written about coaching. They describe the payoffs and skills required to be a good coach. However, it takes two to tango. Virtually nothing has been written about the other side of the equation—the receptivity of the person being coached.

This is a brilliant book, illuminating and providing answers about a huge void in the literature of leadership development and talent management.

Using his 34 years as a highly successful CLO, and now a university fellow teaching executive MBA's, the author shares penetrating insights into the causes of all leaders' success or failure. It boils down to leaders seeking and responding to feedback. But beyond making a compelling case for the importance of this behavior, practical ways to make this happen are provided.

Coachability: The Leadership Superpower is at once an extremely insightful treatise about a vital capability for new and experienced leaders everywhere. It is also an enormously helpful gift to all coaches and leadership development professionals.

—John Zenger
CEO, Zenger Folkman

Poignant! One of the most important skills a leader can have is their coachability—yet it's so often overlooked. Learn to ask for ways to improve, grow in your role and be the best leader possible with the tools from *Coachability!*

—Dr. Marshall Goldsmith, Thinkers50 #1 Executive Coach
New York Times best-selling author, *The Earned Life*; *Triggers*,
and *What Got You Here Won't Get You There*

Much has been written about being a coach; almost nothing about being coachable. This marvelous book fills this gap and offers any leader tips on how to seek, respond, reflect, and act on being coachable. Kevin's clever insights and useful tools make this a must-have for leaders today.

—Dave Ulrich, Rensis Likert Professor
Ross School of Business, University of Michigan
Partner, The RBL Group

You can lead a horse to water, but you can't make them drink. This proverb reminds all of us about the reality that others clearly see our strengths and weaknesses that are not visible to ourselves. Want to be more effective, loved, appreciated, feared or admired? Other people can help you, but you need to be coachable. Kevin Wilde unlocks the essential elements of the superpower, Coachability.

—Joe Folkman, President, Zenger Folkman and best-selling author
The Extraordinary Leader, How to Be Extraordinary,
and *The Trifecta of Trust*

In *Coachability*, Kevin Wilde nails the real reasons that promising careers of leaders get derailed. After personally witnessing surprising failures, Kevin uses his vast corporate experience to help today's leaders avoid career trouble and accelerate their impact and growth with practical and proven insight. If you want to succeed as a leader, I recommend reading this book as quickly as possible.

—Kevin Oakes, CEO
Institute for Corporate Productivity and
best-selling author, *Culture Renovation*

Today's world belongs to the most coachable and the most open learners. Kevin Wilde, in his pragmatic book, 'Coachability: The Leadership

Superpower,' gives you tools to grow and to succeed in today's hyper-learning-rich world.

—Kevin Cashman, best-selling author,
Leadership from the Inside Out and *The Pause Principle*
Global Co-Leader, CEO & Enterprise Leader Development at Korn Ferry

Kevin Wilde has identified the simple but subtle and powerful factors that can limit a senior professional's growth and career, and how to transcend them. Implementing any one of his dozens of great suggestions, though not difficult, could be game-changing.

—David Allen, best-selling author,
Getting Things Done: the Art of Stress-Free Productivity

Kevin Wilde has tapped into a critical and often overlooked element of leadership, coachability. I have witnessed the power of coachable leaders as they have expanded their careers, and the derailment of leaders who have been unaware of leadership blind spots. Kevin brings this to light in an engaging, thoughtful, and practical manner. His experience as a successful business leader in Fortune 100 companies, a rigorous researcher, and a teacher of executive MBA's provides him great credibility. Kevin combines real life business experience with meaningful data and an academia approach to learning in a refreshing presentation. This is a book that can both accelerate a leader's career and reignite a leader's career with practical knowledge, awareness, and instruction. This is a must-read for aspiring leaders at all levels and coaches of leaders.

—Mark Urdahl, CEO, Red Wing Shoes

This masterful book offers nothing less than a radical rethinking of the essential practices to becoming a trusted, purpose-focused leader. The ultimate leadership challenge, today, is self-leadership. This must-read book is a voice of realism and a hands-on guide to, first, leading yourself.

—Richard Leider
International best-selling author,
The Power of Purpose, Repacking Your Bags,
and *Who Do You Want to Be When You Grow Old?*

What's one of the most dangerous leadership career derailers? Losing your coachability. Kevin Wilde's new book offers practical and evidence-based ways that leaders at all stages of their careers can sharpen and preserve their coachability superpower.

—Dr. John Boudreau, Professor Emeritus and Senior Research Scientist, Center for Effective Organizations, University of Southern California

Kevin Wilde's book *Coachability* spotlights a critical issue in leadership: are you ready to learn? In an easy-to-use format, this book gives you tips, ideas, and examples that teach you a very important lesson: when you're ready to be coached, you will continuously improve and grow.

—Josh Bersin, Global Industry Analyst HR, Business Leadership, corporate L&D, recruiting and HR Technology

When leaders move up the proverbial organizational ladder, they can easily become overly full of themselves and even a little arrogant, believing they really don't need that much help. Often, they don't see the need for feedback; and even those that do don't know how to take advantage of it, typically resulting in a quick path to derailment and failure. But, being open to feedback and knowing how to learn from it are two different challenges, even though one must precede the other. Kevin Wilde shows how openness to being coached and willingness to take action from it, i.e. coachability, are perhaps the two most critical skills a leader can have if they are going to effectively continue to shine in their roles. He should know given his illustrious career as a human resources executive and Chief Learning Officer at major Fortune 100 companies promoting and installing leadership programming for over 35 years. He adeptly cuts to the chase in providing not only convincing evidence for both the mindset and skillset required, but also providing the tools leaders need to become more coachable. This is a reference that current and aspiring leaders absolutely can't do without.

—Dr. Stephen L. Cohen Principal & Founder, Strategic Leadership Collaborative, author, *12 Winning Strategies for Building a Talent Development Firm: An Action Planning Guide*

Kevin combines the wisdom from 3+ decades with the Generals—General Electric and General Mills—with the discipline/tenacity of an ultra-marathoner to create a must-read for anyone who aspires to lead a company. Thank you for creating and sharing this gift.

—Jeff Prouty, Chairman and Founder, The Prouty Project

This terrific book provides the techniques and the mindset to accelerate your professional development, to be a more empathic leader, and to inspire those around you. Leading in the future will require to be more open in the present. Be coachable, your career depends on it. This book is your starting point!

—Dr. Jason W. Womack
Assistant Professor, Air University, Maxwell Air Force Base
best-selling author, *Your Best Just Got Better* and *Get Momentum*

I love Kevin's research-based and practical approach to outlining why coachability is a needed critical ingredient to help leaders thrive and accelerate their impact and career growth.

—Diana Thomas
Executive Coach, Author & Former Vice President,
Learning & Education, McDonald's Corporation

Today the growing consensus is that what it takes to be a great manager, a great leader has changed. All of us are on a new, steeper learning curve. This book offers a way forward, a well-researched and practical set of tools we can use to take charge of our own development.

—John W. Cone, Chair of the Chief Learning Officer Talent Board/Institute for Corporate Productivity and Chief Talent Development Next Board/Association for Talent Development, former VP of Dell Learning

Coachability: the Leadership Superpower fills a critical need for any leader during this disruptive time period. I like how the book balances building a strong case for being coachable and then providing tools for practical application. With 24 different strategies, there's something for every leader in here!

—Matt Donovan
Chief Learning and Innovation Officer
GP Strategies

As an executive coach, I often feel "responsible" for ensuring that my clients implement important changes. Kevin's premise of the leader's superpower is both obvious and eye-opening: a leader's coachability is one of the greatest determinants of their overall effectiveness. The pragmatic exercises and frameworks presented in this book offer leaders—and the coaches who work with them—an array of choices to enable greater coachability and leadership success. This book clearly represents the many years of Kevin's well-earned experience, research, and wisdom. Whether you are a new leader or seasoned executive, an executive coach or an HR business partner, you will discover valuable practices you can apply immediately.

Kathleen Stinnett, MCC
best-selling author, T*he Extraordinary Coach*
Founder of FutureLaunch

Kevin Wilde has done extensive study into how executives value, ask for, internalize, reflect on, and act upon feedback. Those who lack the vital skill of coachability are flying blind. This book is a great guide, as vital to senior leaders as well as those who are early in their careers.

—Steve Moss, CEO
Executive Springboard

Wilde provides compelling insights and practical guidance for leaders who want to improve their coachability. Every leader can benefit from Coachability—from newbie to executive!

Marc Effron, President
The Talent Strategy Group and best-selling author,
One Page Talent Management

Today's workforce expects leaders who are introspective, use feedback for self-improvement, and understand how their personal growth impacts the people around them. *Coachability: The Leadership Superpower* is a timely title for any leader seeking greater effectiveness in their role and any employer tasked with accelerating leadership development in their organization. Wilde's four essential practices of a coachable leader—seek, respond, reflect, and act—help readers remain lifelong learners at any point in their career journey.

—Ann Parker,
Associate Director, Talent Leader Consortiums,
Association for Talent Development (ATD)

Truly great coaches are a rare breed, but not so rare as truly coachable leaders—and it is those leaders that have an unfair advantage over the others. *Coachability* seeks to level that playing field with highly-practical takeaways that all leaders can learn from. This is the book that can help you!

—Rich Mulholland
Founder Missing Link: Presentation Powerhouse and
Author, *Boredom Slayer*, *Legacide* and *Here Be Dragons*

Never more than today do organizations need leaders who work in a learning zone. They seek and respond to feedback, reflect on what they learn, and act based on their learnings. Kevin's timely book is a practical and engaging resource for people who want to deliver results by taking advantage of the superpower called leadership.

—Patti P. Phillips, Ph.D.
CEO, ROI Institute

This is a wonderful book that makes a very simple point. Coaching is only effective if the coachee is coachable. This is no glib statement but a profound insight. My book shelves groan under the weight of books on coaching: what it is, how to do it, how to measure its effectiveness, and so on. There is only one book on coachability and that is the one by Kevin Wilde.

There is a simple equation that underpins this book: the more senior you are the more likely you are to have a coach; the more senior you are the less likely you are to open up to being coached effectively. I cannot think of anyone I know who would not benefit from reading this short book. In less than 200 pages, Kevin nails so many of the blockers that prevent us stepping forward in our leadership and upward in our careers. He offers insight after insight of behaviors that consciously or (often) unconsciously shut out the key coaching messages and he reveals the defenses that we erect to make ourselves almost uncoachable.

As a coach I have seen those barriers descend like medieval portcullises, and I have found it hard to reverse that process. As both a coach and a coachee the insights from this book are genuinely groundbreaking, accessible, and powerful. It should be mandatory reading for leaders at all levels in all organizations. It is impossible not to have your eyes opened. It will make you much more coachable, but more than that, it will open you up to challenging some pretty fundamental assumptions and, therefore, help you on the vital path to becoming a lifelong learner that gets better and better at both leadership and followership."

—Nigel Paine, speaker, author, and broadcaster on corporate learning;
former Head of BBC's Learning and Development Operations

Use this book to put yourself in the "coachability zone." Kevin Wilde's work-life based examples, techniques, and templates will generate insights that stimulate your professional growth and development. Highly recommended if you are preparing for a formal coaching engagement; essential if you are determined to gather meaningful input from others to increase your leadership effectiveness.

—Francois Raymond
Global Talent Development and Coaching Services Mgr,
Ford Motor Company

Managing amid constant and increasingly unpredictable change is a leadership imperative. This demands and rewards those who desire and demonstrate the ability to continuously learn and adapt; in essence, they are coachable! No one knows this better than Kevin Wilde who artfully blends research with deep empirical wisdom and pragmatic tools in this essential guidebook for those who seek to lead in this new era of work.

—Kevin Martin, Chief Research Officer,
Institute for Corporate Productivity

Coachability:
The Leadership Superpower

Kevin D. Wilde
https://www.thecoachableleader.com

Illustrations by Becca Hart
Edited by Courtney King Bain

ISBN 13: 978-1-64343-719-4
Library of Congress Catalog Number: 2022913807
Printed in the United States of America

First Printing: 2022
25   25   24   23   22   5   4   3   2   1

Book design and typesetting by Tina Brackins.
This book is typeset in Caslon and Fira Sans.

Pond Reads Press
939 Seventh Street West
Saint Paul, MN 55102
(952) 829-8818
www.BeaversPondPress.com

To order, visit **https://www.thecoachableleader.com**.
Reseller discounts available.

Contents

Part I: The Case for Coachability

Part II: How to Be a Highly Coachable Leader

Foreword

A Confession

I've had coaches for most of the last thirty years.

On the one hand, I can clearly see how they've contributed to the various successes I've had. They've helped me think smarter about challenges I faced. Coaching has helped me uncover things I would otherwise have missed, be a wiser leader to my direct and indirect reports, and change some of the patterns of behavior that would have hindered rather than helped.

On the other hand—and this is embarrassing to admit—I can also clearly see how much additional opportunity and potential for the impact I frittered away for this single reason: I didn't know how to be coached.

It's an odd thing to admit.

I mean, how hard is it to be coached? Surely you just . . . show up, and the magic happens?

The clue to the mistake I made (and you might be making too) is the passive nature of the verb: "be coached." It lulls you into a false sense of complacency. You're going to be pushed, cajoled, encouraged, cheered on, provoked, supported, and so on. The coach does all the work. You just reap the benefits.

That's a recipe for a disappointing experience. And that's a terrible waste of time, money, and possibilities.

A Journey Ahead

This book's author, Kevin Wilde, would wholeheartedly agree. I first met Kevin when visiting General Mills years ago. I was struck by the development culture of the place and noted Kevin's passion for unlocking the potential of great learners and leaders at all levels. In fact, things were going well there, with lots of kudos as a "best of" company for leadership learning and even a "Chief Learning Officer of the Year" honor.

Yet I could sense Kevin was not satisfied and was on a journey to figure out a missing piece about leadership development. He has since uncovered what I had experienced—it's not just about taking a leadership training program or being coached.

It's about your coachability.

This book is the result of that journey. It lays out a compelling case for you to step back and think about your level of coachability to avoid the waste and loss of potential growth. The first part of the book provides the "why" and "what" of coachability, backed by research and experience. The second half is a pragmatic and valuable guide for the "how" of coachability.

This book serves as a great resource to help you on your growth journey. As you start down the path, consider three decisions:

Decide to resist the resistance

Weirdly, the very act of being offered help creates resistance to that help.

If you're successful (and I'm sure you are), you'll find resistance to any feedback or coaching. After all, look how far you've already come.

And if you're struggling (and I'm sure at times you are), you'll find resistance to that feedback or coaching. You don't want help, you don't want to see your role in the mess, you don't want to break familiar patterns.

I find the question "How much risk am I willing to take?", or its sister question, "How vulnerable am I willing to be?" to be helpful. They invite me back into the light to choose openness and willingness.

Noticing and managing the resistance unlocks the power of your coachability.

Decide to respond to the responsibility

When someone gives you feedback or offers some coaching, there is a strong inclination to hand the full responsibility for the value of the message or mentoring to the other person. Likewise, the lack of others providing helpful observations or development support can lull us into a false sense that they would tell me—rescue me—if it mattered.

Instead, respond with your very best skills to understand what's offered. And reach out for feedback and help if it's lacking. Resist the temptation to be solely transactional. Consider it a chance to create and contribute to growing your potential.

Decide to read this book for action

A great leader today is both a coach and coachable. This book can help you elevate your responsibility for growth and establish new habits for capturing more of those coachable moments that matter so much in our lives. Each chapter offers terrific insights to consider and practical tools to try out. So, grab a pen to take notes for action and turn the page now to begin your journey of leadership coachability!

—Michael Bungay Stanier
Best-selling author of *The Coaching Habit* and *How to Begin*

First Words

Please Begin by Leaving the Room

Imagine you are wandering through a room full of strangers, desperately seeking your phone. You are puzzled as to why no one is responding to your pleads for help. You realize you are on your own. Your heart starts beating faster as you dart around the room. Still no luck. Suddenly the room explodes with useless chatter. Your frustration grows as you stop and wonder what the heck is going on. You now regret volunteering for this in the first place.

Welcome to the opening moments of my leader coachability workshop. The session starts by asking someone to step out of the room momentarily but to leave their phone behind. Upon reentry, I tell the volunteer to find their now-hidden phone. The exercise is timed. At first, the volunteer starts roaming around the room, a bit confused and annoyed that no one is helping or even responding to requests for clues. Then, after thirty seconds, the room comes alive as people start "helping" by offering such encouragements as:

"You are really working hard at finding your phone! What a great growth mindset!"

"I admire your willingness to jump in and volunteer."

"I bet you'll find that phone soon enough and, by the way, love those shoes you are wearing. Where did you get them?"

At first, all the positive comments energize the volunteer, and the search pace doubles, until it sinks in that all that positive buzz isn't helpful. Another thirty seconds go by, and the group suddenly shifts into shouting out, "Warmer, warmer" or "Colder, colder" as the volunteer moves around. Realizing we are now playing an old childhood game, the volunteer moves intently to elicit the "warmer" calls and away from the "colder" ones. Within the next thirty seconds, the phone is found hidden under a name tent, third row on the left side (hint: this is where I always hide the phone). In the many years of running this introductory test, no one has found the phone before the warmer/colder feedback begins.

As the exercise ends, I explain that the group was instructed to first stay silent, then to provide positive yet generic encouragement, and then finally to provide meaningful feedback by shouting out "warmer" if closer to the phone and "colder" if moving away from it.

Have you ever felt like the phone-seeking volunteer? You have a job to lead and earnestly go about doing it. You move frantically from here to there with an air of determination and self-confidence, hoping you are on track. At times when things feel cold, you'd appreciate some direction and coaching. But for some reason, you hesitate to ask for help, or you can't make sense of what you are hearing. Your frantic pace increases, getting you even further off track. You may even wonder why you chose to lead in the first place.

Are You Getting Warmer or Colder?

The Warmer/Colder exercise is an introduction to keeping your career on track and remaining coachable. "Warmer" for what you are doing well and should continue doing, and "Colder" for what you aren't doing as well and need to do something different. As I started to collect research on remaining coachable, two findings stood out: (1) we warm up to faulty leadership assumptions, and (2) the habit of seeking help and self-improvement grows cold.

We tend to lose our formerly strong feedback and coach-seeking habits as we get older and advance in a career. As a result, we have a harder time being as positive and effective as we can be and, in some cases, develop blind spots that may take us off the career track, heading for derailment. Originally this book was going to be about derailment. But that's just reporting on the accident. I realized that knowing how to avoid the accident is much more valuable. And that's coachability.

Every year billions of dollars and millions of training and coaching hours are spent in pursuit of developing leaders. So why is it CEOs still complain that a lack of sufficient leadership talent continues to be a top threat to business success?* Perhaps helping leaders warm up their coachability would keep the training and coaching investments on track.

Originally this book was going to be about career derailment. But that's just reporting on the accident. Knowing how to avoid the accident is much more valuable, and that's coachability.

Leaders On and Off the Track

Helping leaders grow is the heart of my career journey, and I hope you'll find this book useful for your growth as well. This book is drawn from my experience with leaders and their development from a variety of organizations in my over forty-year career. I believe what I've learned will help you, whether you are early or later in your career, work in a large global corporation, a small start-up,

---

*See the Reference Notes section at the end of this book for source references if you are interested in tracking down the details. You can also check the latest findings on my website, **www.thecoachableleader.com**.

or a community-based organization.

My trip through corporate life started with seventeen years at General Electric in a couple of divisions, and then at the global corporate leadership training center. This was followed by seventeen years as the senior talent development executive at General Mills. Now, for more than a half-dozen years, I serve as an executive leadership fellow at the business school for the University of Minnesota, where I teach and research leadership in the executive MBA and Supply Chain Management programs. I also provide individual leader coaching and organization training programs. And at every step of the journey, I've worked to personally apply the lessons of leadership, sometimes well and other times falling short. (More on that later.) All in all, the lessons keep coming, and I continue to see myself as a student of the game of leadership.

One lesson stands out. While developing leaders at General Mills, I would meet regularly with the CEO and top team to review the state of our leaders. These meetings were always a highlight for me, as the conversations were lively and important to these business leaders. Those were heady days, as the company's performance was on a roll, and we were filling a trophy case with awards for "best of" leadership development. With all that success, I was nervous to report one time on leadership failure. While typically reporting on a wealth of talented and up-and-coming leaders, I gingerly introduced a study of formerly star leaders who didn't work out and were terminated. (Spoiler alert: the loss of coachability emerged as the main derailment pattern.) The meeting went better than expected, yet our development efforts were falling short of keeping the stars shining.

An Invitation to Explore Your Own Coachability

This book is about leading with a Warmer/Colder approach—a mindset and set of practices called leader coachability. The goal is to regain that early-career habit to learn more, to be more coachable, and to expand your leadership effectiveness and career potential. You'll find what follows to be a blend of notable research, best-practice strategies, and stories of leaders on all parts of the coachability spectrum. You'll read some of my own stories mostly on the wrong side of that spectrum.

In Part I, you'll be introduced to the connection between low coachability, blind spots, and faulty assumptions that contribute to career derailment. You'll see research that points out the power—the superpower—of being highly coachable, a skill set highly prized in an era of constant change demanding agile learners at all levels. From the research and study of highly coachable leaders, you'll find a pragmatic roadmap of coachability and the four practices that matter most.

Part II chapters explore each core practice. You'll find stories and lessons from leaders-in-action, offering advice and strategies for your own coachability habit-building. Each story draws from my experiences over the years with leaders in my professional corporate career, coaching, graduate school teaching, and interviews with executive coaches. (I've altered the names and some of the specifics to respect their confidentiality.)

Pause and Take Note

I invite you to take an active role as you read the stories and consider the research. Make it a DIY project by having a notebook at your side as you read. Title it Coachability Notebook and take time after every chapter to write down what you thought was most relevant to you. Each chapter ends with a Pause and Take Note section with summary ideas, questions, and exercises to try.

This book is intended to help you no matter your career stage, training, or experience. The aim is to establish the case for coachability and provide you with credible research and practical insights, with simple tactics to practice. So let's begin with a story of how an unexpected exercise among mingling leaders sparked the investigation of leadership failures and coachability.

Part I:
The Case for Coachability

"Hey, could everybody please stand up . . ."

So the trouble began one day, kindling a mingle mystery and then sparking an investigation of the risks, upsides, and practices of leadership coachability. This section will help you recognize and avoid an all-too-common leadership trap, discover the mounting evidence of why coachability matters today, and see the complete picture of the forces and practices of highly coachable leaders.

Chapter One: Is Derailment in Your Future?

Find out what happened after everyone stood up, the story of good leaders falling off the track, and the one question that predicted it. Meet the five faulty assumptions driving career derailment and the common decline to avoid.

Chapter Two: The Power of Coachability

Examine the clues that unraveled the mingle mystery, why there isn't a straight answer to the question of confidence versus coachability, and why feedback is a problem. Explore the importance of rezoning your mindset while leading.

Chapter Three: Your Coachability Roadmap

Consider the roadmap of coachability, how the environment and personality helps or hinders, and the four essential practices to strengthen your coachability.

CHAPTER ONE

Is Derailment in Your Future?

The Coachability Mingle Mystery

What was unfolding before my eyes wasn't what I expected. Having booked a world-famous leadership coach to speak to my company's top executives, I settled into my chair, expecting a benign lecture on management trends.

The guru had a different idea, and it was unsettling.

"Hey, could everyone stand up," he started. *"Now, think of something you'd like to improve about yourself and move about the room asking people for their ideas."*

Everyone slowly started rising. I caught a cold stare from Mark, my boss, seemingly to signal that we don't do things like this here. The company culture was polite and orderly. Meetings were orchestrated so no one ever felt uncomfortable. This spontaneous exercise prodding leaders to share their weaknesses was not polite and quite out of order. I started to worry he thought this was *my* idea.

"Be sure to write down what everyone tells you and say 'thank you' when they are done," Dr. Guru added.

Everyone dutifully found a partner. After a few minutes of asking and offering ideas, they turned to find someone else as the mingling continued. Soon the conversations grew louder, with a few punctuated by laughter. People seemed to be enjoying themselves. After fifteen minutes, time was called, and everyone returned to their chairs.

Dr. Guru asked everyone to shout out a word on what they thought about the exercise. The group quickly replied with:

"Interesting"
"Useful"
"Insightful"
"Fun"

And my inner voice added *relieved*, until a bit later when the confusion started.

Useful, but Never Again

As I bumped into some of the attendees later that week, the post-event buzz was positive. One executive said he picked up tips on how to improve his collaboration with peers; another felt good about ideas to improve her prioritization effort. Later I heard one leader met with the CEO to continue the conversation from the mingle.

At the time, I thought all was well and provided a personal learning event for the team. You may have experienced similar "coachable moments" in your career, where you benefited from seeking and receiving valuable advice. And, if you are like me, you probably have other times when it was much harder to act as a coachable leader.

Before we go further, let's define a *coachable leader* and *coachability*:

> A coachable leader values self-improvement and operates consistently in a learning zone by applying the coachability practices of seek - respond - reflect - act.

My hope is that this book inspires your next coachable moment and personal growth. Reading it tells me you value self-improvement and are curious about coachability. You may be wondering if it's worth it. The research you'll see later shows that nurturing a coachability habit increases your leadership effectiveness and career success. It can help you avoid blind spots and faulty assumptions, which can stall your career or derail you completely. You'll become clearer on your learning zone and how certain coachability practices will keep you there. You'll read how the best leaders do it—regardless of level or circumstances—and learn from how others regained their coachability.

More on the zone and practices in a bit; let's go back to the head-scratcher mystery from the mingle exercise.

Given the positive reaction, I assumed the mingle would spark interest in further senior leadership events. But I found quite the opposite. In fact, there was no desire to ever repeat the mingle exercise in any form, even later when shown evidence of blind spots and faulty assumptions in the ranks. Only later did the mystery start to unravel.

Leaders Derailing in our Midst

A month after the mingle event, I met with the CEO and top-dozen executives for an annual talent review. To the team's relief, a mingle was not on the agenda. The main topic was a review of the performance and potential of our top-500 leaders worldwide. The tone was very upbeat at the time, as the company was doing well and, in fact, we were receiving a good deal of external recognition. I recall *Fortune* magazine had just named us one of the best companies for leadership development. Similar kudos were coming from *Chief Executive* magazine, the Conference Board, Inc., and other organizations and publications.

Yet, for the first time, there was something not-so-positive to address. In addition to tracking the success and upward potential of the top-500 leaders, I analyzed leaders who were failing. They were talented, hard-working people we believed in, developed, and promoted, but they were now falling off the career track. The list of derailing leaders wasn't as long as the successful ones, yet it was significant. We needed to understand what was going on. I worried about how the executives would react to the report and wondered whether I could have done more to help the struggling leaders.

Searching for clues on what went wrong, I conducted a post-mortem by interviewing the failed leader's manager and dug into their personnel files. I encountered a fair amount of resistance during these interviews, as most "polite" organizations don't dwell on leadership failure. They'd rather move on and pretend it never happened. Yet, what I uncovered proved valuable to help avoid future career crashes.

Two findings provided the most insight into what was going on. First, it was common for the derailing leader's boss to report that while they knew their employee was on the path to derailment, the failing leader didn't recognize it and had significant blind spots. Second, a review of their last 360 report—a survey of peers, direct reports, and their boss's ratings of their competence and behaviors—pointed to a potential root cause. One survey item showed a significant gap between our successful leaders and the derailing ones:

"Does this leader seek and respond to feedback?"

Derailing leaders were rated thirty percent lower, which most likely contributed to their blind spots in acting with others. During the follow-up interview, managers would often admit that these people were hardly coachable. No wonder the boss saw the upcoming derailment but the uncoachable leader was clueless! I started to keep a list of insights as the investigation continued, starting with:

Low coachability increases blind spots and contributes to career derailment.

To my relief, the senior executives found the derailment findings about blind spots and low coachability intriguing. They agreed to help our leaders receive more training and tools to up their coachability levels. Yet, they continued to show a general lack of interest in investing sufficiently in their own growth. Is it just that some people are more coachable than others? Or is it that an executive coach in a conference room on a particular day can make feedback OK, but, back in the day-to-day workplace grind, feedback isn't so *useful, insightful,* or *fun*? Only later did I uncover what was going on.

The Coachability Decline and Five Faulty Assumptions

Since 2015, I've been trying to understand career derailment, the dynamics of leader coachability, and what can be done to avoid failure. The first finding emerged from Zenger-Folkman, the consulting firm we used for our leadership development assessments. Using their "seeks-and-responds to feedback" survey items, we created a coachability index and analyzed their global data set of over fifty thousand leaders. The results found early-career leaders are seen as very coachable—rated well over seventy percent positive. Unfortunately, the ratings declined steadily at the middle and senior levels. The most senior leaders were rated less than fifty percent positive in their coachability behaviors. Compared to supervisors, senior executives were rated thirty-six percent lower in coachability. The study identified a similar decline by age, regardless of leader level. I also found another meta-study of thirty years of feedback-seeking research confirming this decrease with age and job tenure. If you believe the research, our best coachable days may be behind us, and tomorrow will be lower than today, unless we start thinking differently.

Leaders are commonly seen as less coachable as they advance or age.

Our thinking as leaders may be driving the decline. As I continued researching derailment and coaching leaders, a pattern of limiting beliefs kept surfacing. I call the most dangerous the "five faulty assumptions" that all leaders face as we advance or settle into a role. It begins when we think we are done.

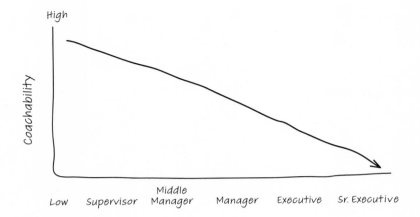

Five Faulty Assumptions of Low-Coachable Leaders

False Finish Line
Superhuman Stance
Boss-Booster Bubble
Lonely Leader Lament
Magic Moment Mirage

False Finish Line

Mason and I met soon after his promotion to divisional president. This move was a big step up, and he was searching for how to transition well. He was open to what I had to say until I suggested checking in with the new team early to solicit feedback and improvement ideas. He pushed back with, *"I've achieved this promotion based on what I've done and what I know. Why would I need to ask my new employees what to do?"* I agreed that his efforts and talent had brought him this far, and he'd earned the big job. But arriving at and performing at the new level shouldn't be confused with each other. It's a false finish line. Further, ongoing learning would be essential for success with such a leap in responsibility, and his new staff could help.

Superhuman Stance

"What would people think if I started asking for help? Would they see me as weak and bewildered?" As an R&D director, Jen worried that others would lose confidence in her technical know-how and thought-leadership. She misread the organization's high-performance culture as expecting perfection and judging any interest in learning to improve as a sign of weakness. Her hesitation was based on the faulty assumption that competent leaders rarely ask for personal-improvement tips and should always maintain a confident "knowing" status—the superhuman, all-knowing stance. Yet the dangers of blind spots and mistaken perceptions lurk for leaders who don't keep asking and learning.

Boss-Booster Bubble

Tonya, a high-potential talent in one of my Executive MBA classes, affirmed the value of listening to others. "I get plenty of feedback about me and, candidly, it's quite positive," she said. Knowing her abilities, I agreed that there was merit in what she was hearing. But I asked her whether most leaders hear the *whole story* of their actions. The boss has more power and status, so those around them become cautious. People start filtering comments. "Do you think people are anxious to please their boss with just the good news?" I asked. Savvy leaders know to probe for more and avoid being seduced in a bubble of booster flattery. As one newly appointed manager told his team in the first staff meeting, "I don't want to hear only the good news; I want to hear the whole story—good and bad."

Lonely Leader Lament

Leaders are often advised to separate from the old peer group when promoted. You can remain friendly and approachable, but you need to establish yourself as a leader—not their buddy. Kelsey experienced the unintended consequence of losing her old gang—fewer people to informally tell her what's happening and how she was coming across. As a supply chain department leader, she also recognized that her new colleagues were quite busy with their responsibilities and rarely connected. She felt the lonely leader lament and needed to find new learning relationships. Kelsey forged new connections with monthly breakfast get-togethers with other supply chain leaders in the city. She also found an internal mentor who served as her trusted advisor and truth-teller.

Magic Moment Mirage

It's not uncommon to hear from people who want to improve their coachability, but just not right now. They say they will work on it as soon as they complete the new corporate initiative, finish the new customer acquisition strategy, onboard the new staff member, etc. The faulty assumption here is that learning can wait, and things will eventually settle down. That's a mirage of a magical moment down the road when the time to learn will appear. We all know more work will appear and good intentions will fade away.

Solving the Mingle Mystery

 surprise mingle exercise pulls a group of leaders back to coachability. But only momentarily. The mystery is why it's so hard to sustain it, given the risks of accumulating blind spots, harboring faulty assumptions, and courting career derailment. I went back for a second look at the Zenger-Folkman 50k leader assessment database, searching for answers, and uncovered evidence of the exception and the power of those who sustained their coachability.

Pause and Take Note

Before moving on to solving the mystery, pause and imagine you and I are having a coaching conversation. Shift from a passive reader to an active learner by starting a journal (physical or digital) to create your own personal Coachability Notebook. I'll begin our conversation at the end of each chapter with a 3-2-1 Summary of key points, questions for you, and an action to take followed by notebook exercises. After every chapter, jot down what ideas struck you as relevant, answer the summary questions, and complete the notebook exercises. As you move through the chapters, you'll be creating a helpful paper trail that will serve as a valuable reference long after you put this book back on the shelf.

(Note: you can access PDF versions of the worksheets for your Coachability Notebook at **www.thecoachableleader.com/notebook**.)

Chapter One: **Is Derailment In Your Future?**
3-2-1 SUMMARY

3 Key Points:

1. Interest in seeking feedback and being coachable declines as we age and advance in our careers. Blind spots emerge, which could contribute to career derailment.

2. Underlying the decline in coachability are five common faulty assumptions: False Finish Line, Superhuman Stance, Boss-Booster Bubble, Lonely Leader Lament, and Magic Moment Mirage.

3. A coachable leader values self-improvement, operates in a learning zone, and applies the coachability practices of seek, respond, reflect, and act.

2 Questions:

1. Have I ever experienced one of the faulty assumptions and what were the consequences?

2. Would I consider myself less coachable than earlier in my life and career, and what are the risks of being less coachable in the future?

1 Next Step:

Create your Coachability Notebook. Write down what was most relevant and interesting from this chapter, answer the *2 Questions*, and complete the following two notebook worksheets: **Faulty Assumption Reflections** and **Blind Spot Experiences**.

Coachability Notebook: RISK

Faulty Assumption Reflections

Based on the risky assumptions leaders unintentionally adopt as their coachability declines, reflect on which of these assumptions might be keeping you from being more coachable.

Five Faulty Assumptions:

False Finish Line	Superhuman Stance	Boss-Booster Bubble
What brought me here is good enough.	Asking for feedback is a sign of weakness.	People only tell positive and pleasing things about me.

Lonely Leader Lament	Magic Moment Mirage
There is no one to learn from at this level.	Once things slow down, I will work on improving.

1. Which faulty assumptions may be part of my thinking now, or might I have experienced in the past?

2. How could these assumptions create blind spots or limit my leadership effectiveness? Check your thinking by talking with a trusted friend, coworker, mentor, or professional coach.

3. What are some ways I can challenge or avoid faulty assumptions thinking as I lead?

For PDF versions of all worksheets, please go to **www.thecoachableleader.com /notebook**

Blind Spot Experiences

We all have blind spots as we go about our daily lives. What matters is to minimize them, especially in areas important for our values and responsibilities. Recall some of your experiences where you recognized or had your eyes opened to a blind spot. Are there any patterns or themes from your experiences, and how can you minimize your blind spots?

1. What were times when you were surprised about how others perceived your actions?

2. Did these situations have any common elements or patterns (e.g., situations, types of people, what you were thinking, what you did or didn't do that contributed)?

3. Are there any current areas where there might be a risk of a surprise or potential blind spot (i.e., something you are ignoring), and what might you do to address these risks?

CHAPTER TWO

The Power of Coachability

Finding the Exception to Decline

N ot everyone follows the declining coachability crowd or buys into faulty assumptions. A relook at the assessment of 50,000 leaders found exceptions to the general downward slide in coachability. This group of leaders had high coachability scores regardless of level or age. Others saw them as exceptional as well. Highly coachable leaders were consistently seen as better and more skillful leaders reflected in top ratings across sixteen critical leadership competencies, including innovation, inspiration, strategy, and collaboration.

> *Highly coachable leaders are recognized as better leaders.*

In fact, the top twenty percent of the most coachable leaders were four times more likely to be rated as highly effective overall

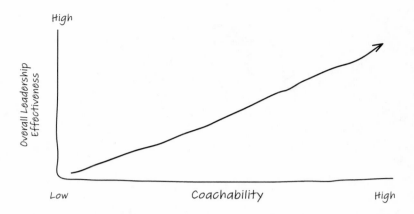

versus the bottom twenty percent.

My investigation found study after study reinforcing the power of coachability. Researchers analyzing a set of over four hundred employees in four major consulting firms found higher levels of creativity and performance from the more coachable consultants—those who regularly engaged in seeking feedback and learning to improve. Another study found highly coachable sales leaders produce greater sales. Coachability also pays off for entrepreneurs. A study found that angel investors are more likely to invest in entrepreneurs who show greater levels of coachability. Investors were saying, "I'll show you the money if you show me you are coachable."

Would you invest your career with a coachable leader? The employees working for highly coachable leader would, based on another finding from the 50k leader assessment. The analysis found two and a half times higher levels of employee motivation and discretionary effort for high- versus low-coachable leaders. Further, good things happen with a leader who has a highly engaged workforce, including higher levels of employee retention, productivity, sales, and customer satisfaction. These teams demonstrated greater adaptability, stronger performance, and even higher promotability potential.

Highly coachable leaders are seen as having greater potential to advance as well. A series of studies uncovered strong links between coachability and a leader's current performance and future advancement potential. One study with nearly five thousand leaders found highly coachable leader performance ratings to be twenty percent higher than their peers. A study of over six hundred leaders found significantly higher promotability ratings for the more coachable ones.

My favorite study compared the coaching skills of the manager versus the coachability of the employees. In looking at over three hundred cases, the coachability of the employee mattered more for higher levels of performance, agility, development, and career potential. While it's good to have both, given a choice to train managers to be better coaches or employees to be more coachable, bet on the power of coachability.

Benefits of a High-Coachable Leader	Risks of a Low-Coachable Leader
Overall leadership effectiveness rated higher	Greater chances of developing and/or expanding blind spots
Higher levels of critical competencies, including innovation, inspiration, strategy, collaboration	Premature career stalling or even derailment
Greater employee engagement and retention	Stuck in old patterns of thinking and acting and loss of opportunities to acquire new skills and abilities
Higher performance ratings	Loss of influence and negative impact on others
Higher promotability ratings	
Greater likelihood of investment support for entrepreneurial ventures	

So, with all the benefits of maintaining high levels of coachability, why do so many leaders fall victim to faulty assumptions and blind spots? On the other hand, if interest in feedback declines with level, please explain the mystery of senior executives enjoying the mingle exercise from Chapter One.

Moving into
The Learning Zone

The mingle mystery started to unravel with one more study. This one looked at three hundred leaders comparing their levels of coachability and self-confidence. The result wasn't a straight line correlating coachability and confidence; it was a curve.

On the low side of confidence, leaders were less likely to be seen as coachable. I called this the "I Can't" zone, where feedback is seen as a threat and should be avoided. On the opposite side is the

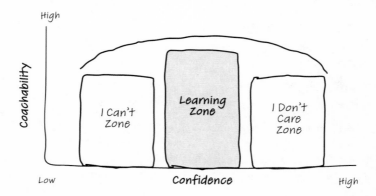

overconfident leader, the "I Don't Care" person who dismisses feedback as irrelevant. Many faulty assumptions are found on either extreme of the confidence spectrum. For example, *"They would doubt me,"* or Superhuman Stance, on the low end of confidence and *"I've arrived,"* or False Finish Line, on the high end. The magic of the coachability curve is the middle: enough confidence to learn more and enough humility to want to. These leaders operated in what I call the "coachable learning zone."

Perhaps the mingle exercise relocated everyone into their learning zone. Instructions set the right amount of confidence. Leaders picked their improvement question of interest. The exercise implied an ethic of humility as everyone was invited to have an improvement question. Everyone did the exercise together, taking turns asking and advising. For that short period of time, everyone seemed to enjoy and benefit from being in the zone. But I later observed that most went back to their "business-as-usual" zone, confirming the challenge of staying in the learning zone.

> Highly coachable leaders live in the coachable learning zone.

Sally Grimes, CEO of Cliff Bars, is an example of a leader who lives in the coachable learning zone. In a recent *Wall Street Journal* profile, she explained what got her there:

"Early on in my career, I had the feeling that I had to be the smartest person in the room coming out of business school and that led to some mistakes," she said. Since then, she said, she learned a key lesson: *"Humility is not the opposite of confidence. It's the freedom for learning."*

Sally was fortunate to discover the right balance of confidence and humility to freely operate in her coachable learning zone, even as a CEO. Unfortunately, for every Sally Grimes, there are more leaders who operate under the influence of faulty assumptions as they advance. They succumb to the downsides of low coachability and miss the power of staying coachable. The reason may have to do with coachability being overlooked.

Why Coachability
is Overlooked

A simple Google Trends search points to why feedback, the learning zone, and coachability tend to get overlooked. The search service invites you to input two terms and returns the current search popularity of each. Try "How to give someone feedback" and "How to receive feedback." Give is the hands-down winner, with a 10:1 ratio of search popularity over receive.

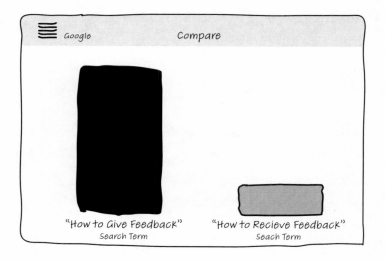

The *give* searchers will find plenty of advice, which also points to the imbalance. I followed a news aggregator service for ninety days, looking for any article or post on the topic of feedback. Far more stories and posts were on giving versus receiving feedback, with such titles as:

"Five ways to give more effective feedback."
"The one thing not to do when giving negative feedback."
"The best strategies to give someone feedback they need."

And on and on. For every nine items on how to tell someone to improve giving feedback, there would be one lonely offering on how to receive feedback well. Now, I recognize the trepidation of not knowing how someone will receive your feedback, so getting a few good tips is appreciated. But a better balance would help. If there were equal interest in skillfully *receiving* feedback, the pressure to give it flawlessly wouldn't be so high. Coachability is overlooked because we are obsessed with delivering the message and not equally learning how to receive it well.

Getting Outranked

Another sign of the imbalance is found in book rankings. While there is an almost uncountable number of books on leadership, there are only a handful about feedback receiving. A recent scan of Amazon book rankings shows the top-three books:

> Thanks for the Feedback – rank #23,254
>
> Feedback (and other Dirty Words) – rank #522,345
>
> Feedback Fundamentals – rank #997,282

At best, 23,253 books outrank the most popular feedback book, and at worst, there are nearly a million books more popular. Being highly skilled at receiving feedback as a leader might be classified as a best-kept secret and not a bestseller.

What isn't a secret is the popularity of studying one's emotional intelligence (EI or EQ). The Daniel Goleman work has spun off dozens of books on the topic and *all* outrank feedback books. EI is commonly defined as the awareness and ability to manage one's emotions as well as recognize the emotions of others. EQ is often used as a related measure of one's interpersonal and communication skills in service of EI. Yet, the popularity might be slightly out of order as indicated by a study of over 5,000 new hires who failed. The top-two reasons were listed as:

#1—Lack of coachability
(twenty-six percent of dismissals)

#2—Lack of emotional intelligence
(twenty-three percent of dismissals)

Interestingly, the research found lack of coachability was cited a bit more often than lack of understanding and managing emotions. Certainly, EI and EQ are valued skill sets for leadership effectiveness. There are some overlapping concepts with the broader framework of coachability, especially attributes of self-awareness and social awareness. Put another way, coachability is a broader leadership framework where the skills of EI help. Yet the ranking gap remains. You'll find plenty of workshops for training leaders in stronger EI skills in the $300+ billion leadership training industry. Likewise, a current hot training topic is "Leader as Coach," with hundreds of how-to workshops teaching coaching steps, asking probing questions, and, yes, offering better ways of *giving* someone feedback. But you'll have a hard time finding a workshop on *receiving* feedback and "Being a More Coachable Leader"!

Feedback-giving versus leadership coachability is out-searched, outranked, and out-trained. So, what is going on? I propose it has a problem with reputation. Despite the cheery encouragement that all feedback is a gift, *it isn't* (with apologies to the authors of *"Where's the Gift? Using Feedback to Work Smarter, Learn Faster and Avoid Disaster"*, Amazon rank #373,212). Most of my workshop attendees admit that the feedback experience is usually akin to being hit on the head with a hammer. Most human beings avoid hammer blows to our noggin and wince every time someone remarks, "Hey, got a minute? I've got some feedback for you," or,

"How about another mingle exercise?" Over time, the faulty assumptions start creeping into our thinking and we drift away from our coachable learning zone.

A Return to Coachability

J ason volunteered to leave the room at the onset of one of my coachability workshops for the warmer/colder exercise, and his return marked the beginning of his coachability comeback. As a driven, hard-charging, always-on sales manager, he energetically chased around the room looking for his hidden phone (if you skipped the Introduction, please refer to it to understand the exercise.) Only after listening to the "warmer/colder" hints did he find success. Then he realized that his frustration of searching aimlessly for his phone matched a growing concern at work. His personal brand of being the driven hotshot who made a difference didn't seem to be panning out in the new organization. Six months into the new job, he wasn't getting support from his peers for his ideas, and in fact, others were working around him rather than involving him in important decisions.

Later in the workshop, the picture of what was going on became clear as Jason reviewed the results of his coachability assessment. (*Note:* you can find a simplified version of the assessment at the end of Chapter Three.) The report scored Jason high on his valuing self-improvement but much lower on many other dimensions. His low scores on seeking feedback and acting were concerning. In the past, these were strong areas, but upon reflection, the faulty assumptions of the False Finish Line and Superhuman Stance were now taking hold of him.

In a follow-up coaching session, he remarked that he had no

interest in being part of my next leader derailment study and shared his turnaround plan. He handed me a worksheet detailing how he would seek feedback, listing two key peers, a potential mentor, and his manager. He spelled out specific questions and how he would approach these people. I invited him to role-play an encounter with me to practice how he was going to respond to feedback. I heard from Jason a few months later. The discussions went well, and he was now working to build stronger relationships and adjust to the new culture. He recognized he had work ahead, but I was encouraged. Jason was returning to the power of his coachable learning zone and would not be another derailed leader case study.

PAUSE AND TAKE NOTE

So how can you get back into your learning zone and tap into the power of being a highly coachable leader? A starting point is knowing your current profile with a precise and comprehensive picture of coachability. You'll find a full picture in the next chapter. But first, please pause and return to your Coachability Notebook, capture your thoughts from this chapter by responding to the following 3-2-1 Summary items and using the **Rezoning Guide** exercise to reflect on your personal coachable learning zone experiences.

Chapter Two: **The Power of Coachability**
3-2-1 SUMMARY

3 Key Points:

1. Some leaders stay coachable regardless of level or age, and reap the benefits, including having stronger skills, more motivated teams, and higher performance and promotability ratings.

2. Coachability is often overlooked as a critical leadership skill, as the interest in giving feedback is more popular than receiving it. Plus, the term feedback has a bad reputation.

3. Coachable leaders operate in their learning zone, balancing enough confidence to learn more and sufficient humility to want to.

2 Questions:

1. What pulls me out of my learning zone and what can I do to pull myself back into the right balance of confidence and curiosity?

2. How might I reframe my thoughts and feelings about feedback?

1 Next Step:

Create a set of guidelines to help you operate in your learning zone by completing the Coachability Notebook worksheet **Rezoning Guide**.

Coachability Notebook: VALUE

Rezoning Guide

Highly coachable leaders work to keep themselves in the "Coachable Learning Zone" with the right balance of confidence, curiosity, and humility. Reflect on (1) your experiences being in and out of the coachable learning zone and (2) what you can do to set up guides to operate more regularly with the optimal balance.

Examples of where I have operated in each zone.

Low Confidence/ Low Coachability (The 'I Can't' Zone)	Right Amount of Confidence, Curiosity, and Humility (The Coachable Learning Zone)	Too Much Confidence, Too Little Curiosity, Low Humility (The 'I Don't Care' Zone)
Examples:	*Examples:*	*Examples:*
Fear of failure, unnecessary self-criticism, fatigued, isolated from others	Challenge that inspires new approaches, positive role models, assume positive intent and not take input personally	Too busy to reflect and learn, little incentive or motivation to be open, rationalizing all feedback as irrelevant or inaccurate

Analysis: What did I do/think that caused me to operate in each zone? How did the situation and what others did/say contribute as well?

Self:	Self:	Self:
Situation/Others:	Situation/Others:	Situation/Others:

Guides: What can I do to remind myself to operate more in the Learning Zone?

Increase Confidence ▶	Maintain Learning Zone	◀ Increase Curiosity and Humility

For PDF versions of all worksheets, please go to **www.thecoachableleader .com/notebook**

CHAPTER THREE

Your Coachability Roadmap

Tell Me a Story

"Tell me about a time you worked with a highly coachable leader as well as with someone who was quite the opposite."

My search to understand coachability began by interviewing fifty executive coaches. Having seen links between coachability, career derailment, and overall leadership effectiveness, I wanted to gain a thorough understanding by uncovering answers to four central questions:

- What does leader coachability look like?
- Do circumstances and environment dictate coachability?
- Is coachability just a trait, with some people having it and some not?
- Can a person do something about it?

The coaches told stories of both high and low coachable leaders, including:

A new leader struggling and looking for help. The workload stress and life pressures were becoming overwhelming. The coaching pause provided a chance to step away from the challenges, acknowledge the lack of organizational support, and figure out a new approach.

A resistant client who was a master of explaining away any bad behavior as a victim of circumstances or others' short-comings. At the end of the coaching, the leader didn't think the coach was much help either.

A chatty supervisor who enjoyed every coaching session, loved exploring new ideas and ways of improving but had a hard time putting ideas into action.

An early coachability roadmap was taking shape as these coaches told their stories. My next step was to expand the search to what's been studied and written about coachability and related notions, including:

- what books and articles are published in the popular press, turning up those low-ranked feedback books mentioned in the previous chapter;
- what is online about leader coachability, namely blogs and postings full of opinions, personal stories, and sports-related stuff, but not much grounded in research or practical organi-zational life; and
- what academics have studied, uncovering interesting nuggets spread out across many fields, such as feedback-seeking behavior, confidence, self-efficacy, emotional intelligence, learning readiness, agility, mindsets, and mindfulness. (The noteworthy findings are listed in the Reference Notes section.)

Finally, it was time to study coachable leaders directly. I drafted a coachability assessment based on what I've learned so far. With the help of my university research friends, an instrument was de-veloped, tested, and normed over two years to strengthen its valid-ity and reliability. Since then, thousands of leaders have taken the assessment, with many of the high-scoring ones becoming case studies to collect best practices. (*Note:* if you are interested in try-ing this assessment and comparing your scores to others, please visit www.thecoachableleader.com).

Through the interviews, reading, and research, the core questions were answered and the picture of leadership coachability came into focus. Some answers were straightforward, and some were surprising.

What Does Leader Coachability Look Like?

C an you picture a highly coachable leader you know?

Andi comes to mind for me. She was a high-energy entrepreneur who cofounded a successful digital learning company. What impressed me was her constant curiosity, not only on a wide range of business and technical topics but how she led and what she could learn to be better.

Her interest in self-improvement was genuine. Even as her organization grew and her days filled more with executive decision-making and less hands-on doing, she found ways to reach out to keep learning regularly. Others noted her willingness to set aside the rush of business to listen carefully when someone gave her advice or passed along an observation about her leadership. You could tell Andi would give serious attention to what she heard, and act based on what she saw as important for herself and the organization. As a result, Andi beat the risk of start-up leaders stalling out and derailing as the organization grew beyond their capabilities. Her remarkable organization was matched by her remarkable coachability.

What I learned about Andi highlights all the parts of what a highly coachable leader looks like. As you review the following roadmap, consider which areas match the highly coachable leaders you have known.

A Roadmap of Coachability

A ll the elements of coachability—from the derailment findings to the coach interviews and related academic research—can be pulled together in a holistic roadmap to help guide your development as a highly coachable leader.

Five parts are within your control: how much you VALUE self-improvement (your mindset to live in your learning zone) and four specific action practices, *SEEK, RESPOND, REFLECT,* and *ACT.*

Two parts are less within your control: the degree to which the environment surrounding you supports or discourages coachability and your underlying personality characteristics.

Here are the parts that make up the roadmap of coachability:

Value

Highly coachable leaders value self-improvement and growth. They value living in their learning zone as they confidently regard themselves as a work-in-progress and not finished perfection. If they have a blind spot, they want to know about it.

Examples of the underlying *value* element include:

- Viewing feedback from others as a learning opportunity.
- Relying on feedback to develop new and enhance current skills.
- Considering feedback from others critical to reaching goals and improving performance.

Low-coachable leaders see themselves as a finished product;

they're not all that interested in improvement ideas from others. They see themselves as "fully grown." They are more concerned about being right and looking smart.

Highly coachable leaders are concerned about learning more and being better. You can recognize highly coachable leaders by the following four powerful practices in action.

Seek

Highly coachable leaders are intentional at regularly seeking input from others on how to improve. They signal that they welcome feedback and ideas for improvement at any time.

Examples of the *seek* dimension include:

- Looking for opportunities to develop new skills or knowledge.
- Seeking advice from colleagues, peers, and mentors.
- Asking their manager for coaching to help improve.

Low-coachable leaders are too busy to ask. They feel there are very few people worth asking. They are concerned about what they might hear and would rather maintain the status quo. They assume if it's important, someone will tell them. They miss the signals from others and catch blind spots instead.

Respond

Whether incoming feedback is a result of asking for it or not, highly coachable leaders respond in an open way. They allow the message to be given uninterrupted and then probe to fully understand it. They show appreciation for the willingness of the other person to offer input.

Examples of the *respond* dimension include:

- Staying attentive and composed when someone gives feedback.
- Expressing curiosity and interest when receiving feedback.
- Signaling respect and gratitude when someone gives feedback or advice.

Low-coachable leaders act defensive and shut down when someone offers feedback or play-act interest and immediately dismiss the input offered as *"their problem, not mine."* They are poor listeners, overexplaining their behavior and offering excuses. They'd rather point out the shortcomings of others. People learn to stop giving feedback as it's not worth the effort and won't do any good.

Reflect

Highly coachable leaders separate the openness and curiosity while receiving feedback from the reflection and analysis of the message. They take the time to think if the feedback has merit and ways to use it to grow. They know they don't have to act on everything they hear, but they will always pause and reflect.

Examples of the *reflect* dimension include:

- Exploring how to use feedback to improve constantly.

- Thinking about how to integrate and apply new learning to all situations.
- Contemplating feedback when considering various alternatives and avenues to move forward.

Low-coachable leaders care little for introspection. They rarely step back to consider what was heard, the spirit it was offered in, or what value it might have. They may *intend* to think more about it, but rarely find the time. Without reflection, they miss the lesson being offered and repeat the same mistake over and over again.

Act

When deciding to act on feedback, highly coachable leaders start with a mindset of experimentation and achievement in small steps. Once momentum builds from early action, they apply sustainability strategies so a new behavior becomes a habit.

Examples of the *act* dimension include:

- Setting specific, incremental goals to accomplish the needed changes for self-improvement.
- Tracking personal progress and growth.
- Sticking with improvement efforts until it becomes a new habit.

Low-coachable leaders are unsure what needs to change or how to go about changing. They look only for a quick fix that doesn't require much thought or effort. They may have good intentions, but they are easily distracted and have trouble following through. They tend to fall back to old, comfortable habits quickly.

Do Circumstances and Environment Dictate Coachability?

E ntrepreneurial leader Andi fashioned an organizational DNA of continuous learning. She set an example and nurtured a culture where it was easy to be a coachable leader. Researchers and executive coaches would agree that what surrounds you will influence your level of coachability. The coachable leader roadmap includes personality attributes and environment factors which influence coachability. (We'll get to the personality stuff in the next section.)

What Helps

Seeing other leaders acting in coachable ways, especially peers, those above you, and others you admire. The popularity of Carol Dweck's *Mindset: The New Psychology of Success* and Brené Brown's courage and vulnerability work have supported such encouraging workplace cultures. Microsoft now tells its leaders to move from a "know it all" style to a "*learn* it all" style. Even Amazon updated its original fourteen values to include "learn and be curious." More than a handful of places are serious about inspiring this growth mindset and learning culture when they select, train, and reward their leaders. Unfortunately, it's not uncommon to be surrounded by the opposite.

What Hinders

Highly competitive, dog-eat-dog, winner-take-all cultures, toxic leaders in charge, and peers who have mastered the faulty assumption mindsets mentioned earlier in this book. Academic research confirms the detrimental effect of a negative environment. People will not seek feedback if they believe it will be misperceived as an act of the insecure, the uncertain, or the incompetent. Research also finds that your immediate supervisor is the most influential as you weigh the cost of seeking feedback.

And of course: National and regional cultures can significantly influence coachability behaviors. The topic is beyond the scope of this book, but further study may be worth your time to understand the nuances and norms of different countries and cultures. You'll find help by investigating the academic research and practical guides about global cultures, and talking to those from other countries. You may have to adjust your '*how*' to seek feedback and to act coachable across the world, but the imperative to learn and grow remains no matter the setting. It may take some translation. For example, cultural experts will advise you to adjust whom you seek feedback from, the directness of that communication, and the accepted territory for improvement advice. Regardless, the '*why*' remains constant—to be effective, address blind spots, and avoid cultural missteps, coachability is a universal leadership power.

Is Coachabililty Just a Trait, with Some People Having it and Some Not?

"Let me be clear as we start. **Not all leaders are coachable!**"

was surprised to hear this caution while interviewing the director of coaching for one of the world's largest and respected leadership development firms. The business model is based on having lots of paying clients. Yet, she believed that some people weren't worth the trouble. I recall a similar comment from the mingle exercise coach from Chapter One who has a money-back guarantee. He bills only when his client improves. When asked how he makes a living, he says he chooses leaders he knows will improve and skips those who won't change. (Imagine being told a famous coach won't work with you because he believes you won't get better? Quite a depressing diagnosis!)

Now that large leadership development firm has been around for fifty years and is doing gangbuster business. The famous executive coach turns down new assignments because of his jam-packed calendar of clients. So the truly uncoachable may be small in number and there is hope for the rest of us. But underlying personality traits and preferences will influence our coachability potential.

What Helps
High levels of. . .

Openness to new experiences: These people can be regarded as "universal learners." Regardless of subject or situation, this is the natural tendency to have a constant curiosity to explore, learn something new, or try something for the first time. Related traits of high creativity and imagination correlate to coachability as well.

Agreeableness and service to others: People who exhibit high agreeableness are warm, friendly, and tactful. Altruism and service to others also correlate well to high levels of coachability. These attributes support the *respond* and *reflect* coachability practices.

Conscientiousness: Is the trait of being naturally thoughtful, with good impulse control and goal-directedness. Conscientiousness links well with the coachability framework roadmap of *seek,* *reflect,* and *act.* However, this trait can also be a deterrent, if combined with the following.

What Hinders

High levels of. . .

The need for security and structure: Being overly concerned with routine, structure, and process and a high need for security negatively correlate with coachability. Perhaps seeking new input from others involves the risk of the unknown (*"What will I hear? What will they think?"*), and the feedback will challenge a safe and comfortable routine.

And sometimes . . .

Drive, competitiveness, and achievement orientation: While naturally "Openness to New Experiences" folks may be regarded as universal learners, high drive leaders may not be interested in getting better about everything. It's usually *one* thing, such as "How do I learn to be better at X so I can achieve Y?" As expected, high drive also tends to do well with the coachability *act* practice.

Confidence vs. humility: As mentioned earlier, there is an optimal balance between these two factors to live in the learning zone. Low confidence deters being open and coachable. Low levels of humility (i.e., excessively high levels of confidence) limit curiosity to improve. The sweet spot in the middle of these two extremes form the optimal learning zone: sufficient confidence to learn and sufficient humility to care to learn.

Interpersonal skills and extroversion: Surprisingly, research findings are mixed on whether high levels of interpersonal skills and extroversion correlate consistently with high coachability. It does seem to help the *seek* and *act* aspects, but not overall coachability. Perhaps other personality factors are at play.

The Complete Roadmap of a Highly Coachable Leader:

While environment and personality can influence your degree of coachability, the more important factors are (1) your *value* mindset, valuing self-improvement and growth; and (2) operating in your coachable learning zone by applying the coachability practices: *seek, respond, reflect,* and *act*.

Can You Do Something About it?

A study of over 3,000 leaders participating in leadership development programs offers encouragement that, yes, you can do something about your coachability. Their coachability profile—as rated by others—improved significantly comparing pre- and post-program assessments. Some improved their coachability by over twenty-seven percent, and all received higher marks for improving overall leadership abilities. "This does demonstrate that leaders can improve their coachability," said researcher Dr. Joe Folkman, "and improvements in coachability help leaders improve on other behaviors." Improving your coachability profile starts with recognizing what surrounds you and your personality tendencies. Some of these things may be helping you right now, and some hindering. If you buy the upside of being highly coachable and wish to avoid the risks of blind spots and faulty assumptions, consider ways to leverage these "helps" and manage those "hinders." You'll find help with the four key practices of highly coachable leaders. The model roadmap of a highly coachable leader in action is someone who continues to:

- *Seek* feedback and ways to improve consistently,
- *Respond* when given feedback openly,
- *Reflect* on the message and its value meaningfully, and
- *Act* on the decision to improve skillfully.

For some of us, especially earlier in our careers, we may be in good shape on these four practices and just need to fine-tune a few parts of our coachability. For most of us, though, we've fallen out of practice and are unintentionally drifting toward being trapped by those faulty assumptions. Either way, once you've clarified your *'why'* for greater coachability, your next job is to adopt new *'how to'* strategies and tools. Help is on the way as the remainder of this book is a collection of insights and best practices from highly coachable leaders.

PAUSE AND TAKE NOTE

Before moving on, please pause and jot a few notes in your Coachability Notebook on this chapter. What struck you as interesting? Write your answers to the "2 Questions" from the 3-2-1 Summary.

Complete the two worksheets, using the "A Brief Coachability Self-Assessment" to establish a baseline of your current coachability profile and "Benefits, Risks, and Focus" to view where you might begin improving. Doing so will help you zero in on the most important ideas and practice strategies offered in Part II of this book.

Chapter Three: **Your Coachability Roadmap**
3-2-1 SUMMARY

3 Key Points:

1. Highly coachable leaders have a mindset of valuing feedback and being open to learning.

2. Environmental factors and personality tendencies can either help or hinder your level of coachability.

3. You can overcome environment and personality by adopting a mindset valuing self-improvement and applying the coachability practices of *seek, respond, reflect,* and *act.*

2 Questions:

1. To what degree do I hold the mindset that values self-improvement, feedback, and advice from others?

2. How might others rate my current coachability habits of *seek, respond, reflect,* and *act?*

1 Next Step:

Complete the **Brief Coachability Self-Assessment** on the next page and the **Benefits, Risks, and Focus** worksheet. From this preliminary assessment, use your Coachability Notebook to identify the most important coachability practices to learn more about and try.

Coachability Notebook: ASSESS

A Brief Coachability Self-Assessment

To help you identify which coachability framework roadmap practices may be most important to your improvement, here is a brief three-step self-assessment tool. (To try the complete Coachability Practices Review self-assessment and benchmark your results against other leaders, see **www.thecoachableleader.com**.)

Step One: Circle the number by the statement that best represents your current actions and habits.

My Action	Never	Rarely	Sometimes	Often	Always
			Frequency		
1. I set specific goals to improve things about myself.	1	2	3	4	5
2. I seek advice from colleagues and peers to get better.	1	2	3	4	5
3. I learn a lot by reflecting on my experiences.	1	2	3	4	5
4. I stay attentive and composed when someone gives me feedback or criticism.	1	2	3	4	5
5. I am good at following through to achieve my self-improvement goals.	1	2	3	4	5
6. I actively seek feedback, even if it may be critical.	1	2	3	4	5
7. I am thoughtful about when is a good time to make personal improvements.	1	2	3	4	5
8. I avoid being defensive or quickly dismissing feedback when given.	1	2	3	4	5
9. I devote time and energy to developing myself based on feedback.	1	2	3	4	5
10. I look for opportunities to develop new skills and abilities.	1	2	3	4	5
11. I think about integrating feedback and applying new learning to improve.	1	2	3	4	5
12. I express curiosity and interest when receiving feedback or criticism.	1	2	3	4	5

Step Two: Enter your scores from each of the twelve statements above and then tally each column.

2 =	4 =	3 =	1 =
6 =	8 =	7 =	5 =
10 =1	12 =	11 =	9 =
Total Sub-Score:	**Total Sub-Score:**	**Total Sub-Score:**	**Total Sub-Score:**
SEEK Chapter	**RESPOND Chapter**	**REFLECT Chapter**	**ACT Chapter**

Step Three: Your lowest scoring column indicates a starting point to increase your coachability. Refer to the relevant chapter and tools that follow. If your scores are about the same, start with the SEEK chapter.

Benefits, Risks, and Focus

Benefits: List two personal benefits of increasing your coachability:

_____

_____

Risks: List two personal risks of what might happen if your coachability declines:

_____

_____

Focus: What is one area of coachability (seek, respond, reflect, act) you want to improve? Why?

_____

_____

Part II:
How to be a highly coachable leader

"But I don't know where to start . . . I'm hitting a wall when I ask . . . It's been so long that I worry people would walk away wondering what was wrong."

This section is your resource guide to overcoming the obstacles and establishing the routines and habits to be a more coachable leader. The following four chapters will provide stories, tactics, and tools of highly coachable leaders. Each chapter is devoted to one of the four essential practices. A total of over twenty-four strategies and a dozen worksheets are offered to help you get started, get unstuck, or get back to your learning zone.

Chapter Four: SEEK—Look in All the Right Places

Discover the seven strategies highly coachable leaders at all levels use to skillfully solicit feedback and improvement ideas. Learn how adding two simple questions and establishing a truth-teller will help catch vital signals usually missed.

Chapter Five: RESPOND—Stop Listening and Start Noting

Consider the truth of feedback, what not to listen to, and how actors can teach us a better approach. Note how a simple routine can replace resistance with curiosity.

Chapter Six: REFLECT—More Than You Think

See how a three-step guide can translate messy feedback into what it means and what you should or shouldn't do about it. Find out how strategic pauses and getting up to a reflective "balcony" are critical appointments for a busy leader.

Chapter Seven: ACT—An Experiment of One

Take a journey with a leader looking to rebalance the odds as she attempts to turn around a failing project and reset her leadership habits. See how five factors stall our good intentions to improve and how "parking downhill" is one of seven enablers to move the odds back into your favor.

CHAPTER FOUR

SEEK:
Look in All the Right Places

The "Yes-But" Dance

A curious dance can break out after one of my talks on coachability. Jen started what I call the "yes-but" dance as we bumped into each other during a three-day conference.

"Hey, I really liked your workshop yesterday, and I totally buy into being coachable and looking for improvement ideas," she began.

"Yes, that's great," I replied, knowing what was to follow.

"But, I've been at a new place for six months now, and every time I go to my boss and ask how I am doing, all I hear is you are doing fine. That's it. I feel stuck."

After another workshop, Mac admitted feeling stuck as well. A more senior manager than Jen, he had been in the role for three years.

"I now realize I've been without solid feedback for some time and would benefit from upping my coachability game," Mac started.

"Yes, that often happens as you move up in rank and get busy," I confirmed.

"But, I don't know where to start," he lamented. "Just coming out and asking what I could do better seems out of character, and I think others would feel uncomfortable—even a bit shocked—and would tell me what they think I want to hear. And they would walk away wondering what was wrong."

Yes, highly coachable leaders value feedback and input. They are intentional at regularly seeking ideas on how to improve and grow. They also signal curiosity and welcome advice at any time. But, how do you do that, either as an early career leader eager to learn or a seasoned pro who has fallen out of practice?

In both cases, stepping out of the "yes-but" dance requires a different rhythm. Change your tune with a new practice to help increase your *seek* behavior. Consider trying out the following strategies.

Seven SEEK Strategies

Starter Topic
Two Questions
After-Action Review+
Mapping It Out
A Truth-Teller
Seeking the Signals
Checking for Updates

Starter Topic

Jen needed to take a different *seek* move. She was asking a general question and getting a general response. Since being highly coachable isn't a common trait in the workplace, supervisors and others aren't used to fielding the *"How am I doing"* query well and may be suspicious of the intent and nervous about the reaction.

"You are doing fine" is the safe answer.

I asked Jen to think about something specific she would like to learn. After a moment of reflection, she said she was curious about what others thought of her weekly customer service reports. The reports took considerable time and effort to pull together each week; she hadn't heard whether they were hitting the mark. Explaining the Starter-Topic seek strategy, I suggested she try the following approach:

"One topic I'm curious about is learning how others think about my weekly customer service reports and where there might be opportunities to fine-tune them. Of course, now that I've been in this position for six months, I'm open to other observations as well."

Getting out of the general *"How am I doing?"* question and posing something specific helps the other person—in this case Jen's boss—respond to something tangible. And by also offering to hear about other observations, Jen is signaling her coachability overall.

I have two cautions for you about using the Starter-Topic technique: first, you need to choose a specific topic you care about and is relevant to your role. Asking something superficial or of casual interest would leave the impression that either you are just going through the motions (and looking for a "You are just fine" reply) or have a hidden agenda.

Second, be sure you are operating out of your learning zone mindset of "curious and confident." Sometimes we ask only looking for compliments. We get disappointed when we hear something short of "You are perfect." While we all need affirmation and confidence-builders from time to time, the coachability practice of *seek* is an openness to learn both what's good and what could be better.

Two Questions

What's good and what could be better is what I call the "Two Questions" (2Q) tactic. This approach was a lifesaver as I started getting pulled into media interviews. I had never received formal media training, yet there I was, taking phone calls from magazine writers and newspaper reporters firing questions at me about the company's approach to developing our leaders. Sometimes these calls went smoothly, and other times they did not.

The 2Q tactic works in a simple, powerful way to elicit specific and valuable input.

I stumbled into the 2Q approach after one call with a *Fortune* magazine reporter. He was crafting a highlight story to accompany their upcoming list of the "best companies for leadership development." We had placed second on *Fortune's* global list, and I found myself sitting in a conference room, looking down at the speakerphone on the table, accompanied by Marty, the corporate communications manager. Marty's role was to ensure the call went well. After pushing the speakerphone's end-call button, I looked up at Marty and asked:

"Before you go, I'm curious about two things," I began. "We probably will be doing more of these interviews, and I'd like to get better. What's one specific thing I did well on this call that I should do again, and what's one thing I can do even better next time?

While I must admit I was fishing for some affirmation, I was sincere in wanting to be mentored by a professional. I heard what I did well and what I could do better that day and worked that post-call mini-coaching session after every new media interview. Over time, I learned how to clarify any question I didn't understand; how to pause and collect my thoughts before speaking; and how to give short, positive answers and examples.

The 2Q tactic works in a simple, powerful way to elicit specific and valuable input, and I now use it in my coaching and teaching. At the end of your next project or meeting, ask:

- What specifically did I do well and should do again?
- What's one thing I can do differently next time that would be even better?

After-Action Review+

Something even better would be needed to help Mac, the senior leader wanting to "up his coachability game." Imagine the strangeness and discomfort his staff would feel if he suddenly started lobbing feedback questions at them. I suggested a familiar management technique—the After-Action Review—and then blending in the 2Q as a plus.

The U.S. Center for Army Lessons Learned is credited with creating the After-Action Review. The Center promotes capturing lessons learned through a structured team meeting after completing any mission or project. Four simple questions are used:

- What were we trying to accomplish (i.e., the objective)?
- What happened?
- Why did it happen?
- What did we learn, and what can we do better next time?

I asked Mac to think about a recent project where he'd played a significant role. He mentioned a new business plan. I suggested Mac use an upcoming staff meeting to apply the After-Action Review coupled with 2Q. After the team reviewed the project in general, Mac could share an interest in learning more about his impact using "did well/do again" and "what would be even better next time." He should let the team know this would be on the agenda so they could prepare for the discussion. If the team needed to warm up to offering feedback, Mac could start this debrief during one-on-one meetings and later use in staff sessions.

Over time, by adding this After-Action Review+ routine to staff meetings and individual check-ins, Mac would find his team getting comfortable providing improvement ideas. Moreover, he would be acting as a role model, adding coachability to his organization's leadership playbook.

Mapping it Out

The Starter Topic, Two Questions, and After-Action Review+ are tactics you can add to your *seek* practice. But first, step back and map out your overall approach. Begin by drawing three columns on a sheet of paper and label them as follows:

Curious About	Sources	Approach

In the Curious About column, brainstorm what you'd like to learn and the feedback or input you are interested in seeking.

In the Sources column, identify who could provide the feedback on your Curious About topics. Or list people with whom you'd generally value their observations and coaching. In the Approach column, write ways to engage the Sources. See the Situation and Sample Questions table for ideas.

Jen—the early career leader—might have completed her worksheet this way:

Curious About	Sources	Approach
Quality and impact of my customer service reports	My manager	Ask at next update meeting
Clarity and professionalism in my project status presentations in monthly department-wide meetings	Trusted department peers	Schedule coffee chat to request input before and after meetings
Gaining exposure in the company for advancement	Mentor	Add topic for monthly mentor meeting

Mapping out a more formal *seek* game plan can increase the quantity and quality of improvement observations and ideas. Aim for a broad set of sources as research reminds us that we tend to limit our feedback-seeking efforts to those like us. This narrows what we can learn. A better plan would be to tap a diverse set of perspectives. Once your columns are complete, share your plan with a trusted colleague as a way of refining it and committing to action. Review and update your plan periodically as your goals change, project priorities shift, and personal interests evolve.

Here's a resource for your map, showing different approaches and questions to use:

Situation	Sample Questions
New job or project start-up	What is most important as I begin this job? How can I leverage my strengths? What weaknesses might need improvement? What might I need to learn about or improve on to be more effective? What parts of my old job or tendencies will I need to stop doing? What new responsibilities should I invest more time in doing?

Continues.

Situation	Sample Questions
Project or job wrap-up	Before moving on to new projects or duties, what did I do well here that I should continue? What would make me even more effective? What do I need to do to improve for the next project or job? Might there be a blind spot or aspect of my behavior I need to think more about and correct?
Mid-effort check-in (work or relationship)	Could you please share with me what you are observing so far that's working well and what I might need to consider doing differently to make my contribution more successful? To help this work conclude well, what's the most important area for me to focus on now? Are there any aspects of my behaviors that need adjustment? Is there something I need to learn or strengthen to finish this assignment well?
Specific input seeking	I'm trying to improve my X (specific) ability right now. Do you have any specific ideas or observations that would help? Concerning X (specific), what I am doing well and should continue, and what could I improve?
General input seeking	I'm taking time to step back and consider my current abilities, contributions, and opportunities to grow. What thoughts do you have that could help me improve and grow to be even better?

A Truth-Teller

My first leadership role as a manufacturing supervisor proved I needed coaching. Back in the days before direct deposit, I had the simple task of handing out paychecks every two weeks. On that first payday, I decided to spice up the ritual of going from workstation to workstation passing out pay envelopes. As I met each employee, I would say such things as:

"Hey, Rick, here's your paycheck. Did you work hard for it this week?"

"Jane, big money in this envelope for you. Try not to spend it all at once."

I thought I would win the award as the funniest supervisor around. Instead, when I finished my rounds, I found Jim—my senior technical lead—at my little supervisor's desk.

"Sit down," Jim began with a half-smile.

"You know, the buzz is that you'll do OK as the new boss." Jim said, "But, I've got to tell you right now, when you pass out paychecks, shut up."

I was shocked and embarrassed, as I thought everyone would appreciate my paycheck comedy. Jim's sit-down with me exposed a blind spot that would have annoyed my employees every two weeks. Jim became my first truth-teller and trusted advisor. I checked in with Jim regularly to hear how I was doing. And if I forgot to ask, I would find Jim at my desk letting me know when I needed to get back on track with the team.

Thanks to Jim, I've always sought a trusted advisor in every job, especially in new organizations and tough roles. At every stage of my work and teaching career, I've found myself listening intently to a truth-teller, spelling out how I was coming across to others and offering ways to improve. My trusted advisors keep me in my learning zone. They boost my confidence to hear the message and prompt my humility to remind me that I am still on the leadership journey.

Add a truth-teller to your *seek* map and check in often so you don't miss important signals along the way.

Seeking the Signals

"I think you just missed our turnoff!"

Either the sign wasn't noticeable, or I wasn't paying attention. Either way, my truth-telling co-pilot pointed out I just passed the new restaurant we were going to. It happens more often than I care to admit, and it reminds me of times I missed the signals as a leader. Nowhere is this more apparent than when moving into a new organization or taking on a stretch assignment. You drive ahead, showcasing your expertise, pressing change, and missing the signals. You should have slowed down and paid more attention to the resistance or taken a different route. Beyond direct messages, highly coachable leaders routinely look for indirect signals to stay on course.

Steve Moss, president of Executive Springboard—a leadership mentoring and onboarding consultancy—tells the story of being called out at a board meeting because he missed a signal. In a prior role as the head of marketing, he was having an informal (he assumed) stroll with Glen, a company board member. Steve recalls a relaxed, wide-ranging discussion as they headed for dinner after visiting the New York Stock Exchange. Steve heard about a puzzling acquisition story about cheesemakers and kitchen countertops mixed in with a dozen other topics.

Three months later, in a formal board meeting, Glen asked if Steve had followed up on his idea about a new product line. Steve stumbled through a weak reply and promised to work on it immediately. He later realized the cheese-and-countertop story was a request and not idle conversation. He had missed an important signal.

Steve now tells his clients to look for signals. *"Sometimes, in our rush and distraction,"* Steve coaches, *"we don't realize someone just gave us advice or a message to consider."* One tip he passes along is to get in the habit of journaling about conversations and reflect on whether there is more to the story. He has three favorite journaling questions:

- What did I hear?
- What did I think was meant?
- Are there implications for what I should be doing?

And I would add one more: *What clarifying question should I have asked?* In my career I've left meetings unsure what was said or what I needed to do. Unfortunately, my ego of trying to look smart prevented asking one more question. One time, I should have asked one more question with my company's CEO. After guest speaking in a leadership program, he casually commented about a follow-up survey. Two months later he asked about the survey results and, just like Steve, I stumbled through a response to get right on it. Since then, I've learned to pause when I am unsure and take the risk of asking for a clearer signal. I found three situations where fuzzy signals call out for one more question:

- The first setting is a **"blue sky" meeting:** someone is thinking out loud and exploring possibilities with uncertain expectation of action. The question to ask is, *"Do you want me to do further work right now with anything we discussed?"* (The question Steve should have asked Glen and I should have asked my CEO.)
- The second setting is the **strategic planning discussion:** someone expects you to bring concrete thoughts and specifics about implementing an idea. The right question to successfully wrap up the meeting is, *"Do you have enough information to give the green light to begin implementation?"*
- The third setting is the **project update check-in:** someone wants to hear about progress as the idea should be in motion. The ending question should be, *"Are you comfortable with our progress right now, or is there more to be done?"*

Steve encourages newly appointed leaders to curate a set of *signal catchers*. These are people who see things you don't notice about your actions or inaction. Signal catchers could include a longtime administrative assistant, a supportive peer, or a trusted employee. Signal catchers know the buzz. People form positive and negative perceptions about you—the buzz—and as executive coach Marty Seldman points out, checking on the buzz regularly is a savvy way to know if your leadership is on course. Your trusted advisors and truth-tellers are another source to check the "buzz."

Checking for Updates

A chat with a signal catcher or truth-teller is like clicking the "check for updates" button on your phone. From browsers to operating systems, it's a setting worth using regularly. Do it, and things run smoothly. Ignore it at your own risk of apps freezing, beloved features not responding, or the dreaded spinning ball of death appearing. Why? Nothing stands still in the digital world. The old app version has a button or two that needs fixing. Your old program needs help working with your new operating system. Or something happened sometime and somewhere that needs attention. Plus, if you are lucky, the update will introduce new features that are even better than what you have now. But you have to *check for updates*. Now imagine a notice popping up on your leader coachability screen:

Leader Notice – Upgrade Available

Your version 2.01 upgrade is now available with the following improvements. Click **here** to pick up the signals.

Bug Fixes:
- Removes tendency to interrupt people when they are speaking.
- Reduces poor listening when employees digress or disagree.

Feature Enhancements:
- Strengthens strategic planning and signal-catching capabilities.
- Improves collaboration with peers for better support.

Nothing stands still in your leadership world. Not seeking feedback and looking for signals is like ignoring the "check for updates" button. In the virtual world, you can select "automatically check for updates" to keep everything working well. In the real world, highly coachable leaders keep themselves up-to-date and working well by regularly looking in all the right places.

PAUSE AND TAKE NOTE

Even though you are in the Coachable Leader in Action section of this book, it's time to stop and pause. Take a moment to return to your Coachability Notebook to capture your thoughts from this

chapter and list the *seek* tactics to try. As with any new skill development, you'll get better with repeated practice. The first attempt may feel a bit uncomfortable, but over time, you'll find the benefits of asking and checking in outweigh any initial awkwardness and concerns. Start by responding to the "2 Questions" from the 3-2-1 Summary and use the exercise worksheets to map out your seek action plan.

Chapter Four: **SEEK**
3-2-1 SUMMARY

3 Key Points:

1. Highly coachable leaders have specific practices they regularly employ to *seek* input and feedback from others. They avoid the generalities of "how am I doing?"

2. Map out a *seek* strategy by identifying improvement topics of interest, potential input sources, and ways to approach a discussion.

3. Increase your awareness of signals and cues from others that you might otherwise miss. Pause to use more clarifying questions and check in with your truth-teller and signal catchers.

2 Questions:

1. What is one topic where increased improvement ideas would help my personal and leadership effectiveness right now?

2. Who could serve as my truth-teller or signal catcher and how can I start the conversation?

1 Next Step:

Try the 2Q tactic with someone this week and journal what you've learned.

Coachability Notebook: SEEK MAPPING

SEEK—Topic, Source, and Approach Map

If you are interested in increasing the amount of feedback and input from others, use this worksheet to map out a plan. Start by identifying the three main areas:

- WHAT feedback you would like to receive (topic).
- WHO are the people to request feedback from (source).
- HOW you will begin (approach).

Write your responses to these questions on the worksheet. Refer to the chapter's Mapping It Out Situation and Sample Questions table for examples. Here are a few more tips to guide you:

- Be clear on your purpose of seeking feedback. The goal may be to solicit affirmation/appreciation, coaching for improvement, or evaluation to align expectations. Stay open and watch out if your intent is only to request affirmation.
- Outline an opening script as you map out your approach. Communicate your purpose upfront in requesting feedback and choose a time and setting that works best for you and your source.
- Identify opportunities to *seek* input. These might be when:
  - a job or project starts up (*What's most important for me to learn and best ways can I contribute?*);
  - a job or project wraps up (*What takeaways are there from this experience so I can do better next time?*);
  - you're in the middle of an effort (*What am I doing well and should continue and what can I do better moving forward?*);
  - you have a specific area or skill to learn (*I'm trying to improve at X. Any ideas?*); or
  - you need general insights (*Is there anything else that could help me grow and improve right now?*).
- Stay open and curious; ask for specifics and examples; take notes and paraphrase what you've heard. Wrap up by thanking your source and tell them you will reflect on what you've heard. Be sure to follow up.

WHAT Topics for feedback and input	WHO Sources	HOW Approach and timing
Example: Improving my listening and empathy with others.	Example: peers, team members, mentors, family, trusted others.	Example: Our next 1:1 update meeting. Coffee check-in.

Next Action Steps:

Truth-Teller Plan

Identify how you can expand your truth-teller network to increase your coach-ability. Who is a current truth-teller you can leverage more often? Who might be someone new who can observe your behaviors and give you honest feed-back and observations? What would *you* be interested in learning from *them*? Start logging your contact opportunities to track your progress.

Role: Truth-teller (current or potential)	**Content:** What can they observe to help? What questions can you ask?	**Action:** How can you increase check-in frequency (if current) or how to establish the relationship (if new)?

Activity Log (date, person, insight, application):

Signal-Seeking Reflections

Think of times when you missed signals from others: what the situational triggers were, what assumptions or behaviors contributed to the miss, and how to better handle similar situations in the future.

Missed Signal Situation Description	What Contributed to Missing the Signals: Situational Trigger? My Assumptions? My Behaviors?	What I Should Have Done

Common Themes and Tendencies From Situations:

Plans to Increase Regular Signal Seeking (journal questions, meet with signal catchers, practice more clarifying questions, etc.):

CHAPTER FIVE

RESPOND: Stop Listening and Start Noting

The Truth About Feedback

"Ho, Ho, Ho!"
—*Santa Claus*

"So, I know this your trademark thing, and I
don't want to tell you how to do it, but . . ."
— *Studio Director, Dailey and Associates,
in "The Santa Sessions"*

Picture Santa Claus delivering his signature line in a recording studio for a holiday promotion. That's the start of an hilarious clip from the ad firm Dailey and Associates. Santa is happy, confident, and thinks he's done.

But then the feedback starts. The studio director tells him that while it's his trademark thing and he doesn't want to tell him what to do, he wants Santa to deliver it again with a bit more smile. Santa does, but then more feedback and more re-recordings.

"Let's make it a little bigger."

Santa tries again.

"That was too big and too many ho's."

Santa now looks frustrated as he attempts a third try.

"You lost a little joviality there. That was evil."

More tries and more feedback now from a gang of studio personnel.

"That's not how I wrote it."

"I don't think you are hitting the alliterations!"

By the end, Santa is mad and reacts in ways that might land him on the naughty list.

So much for feedback. The truth is, while it's touted as "a gift," feedback often feels unhelpful and unwelcome. We all would rather not open that "gift"! But what about those highly coachable leaders? Are they better gift-receivers than the rest of us? Most likely not. But they have learned the secret of not listening and instead taking notes.

Stop Listening Inside

When feedback arrives—either because you asked for it or it just shows up unsolicited—coachable leaders respond by stopping. They stop listening to the negative voices in their head. As authors Douglas Stone and Sheila Heen admit in their book *Thanks for the Feedback*, we seek acceptance and shun anything perceived as threatening … like feedback. Defense mechanisms start kicking in when someone attempts to give us the "gift" of feedback. Two voices in particular start chattering in our minds that sound something like this:

"You don't understand!" This inner voice is complaining that the feedback giver just isn't right. Maybe you didn't do something well, but that was only *one time* compared to the nine previous times when you did it perfectly. Or perhaps that person just doesn't understand the pressures you are under, the missing facts of the situation, or how hard you are trying. Or you just need more sleep/coffee/time/you-name-the-excuse.

"Who are you to tell me that?" This inner voice is wondering when the other person will be done jabbering so you can give *them* the gift of feedback. You'll politely appear as though you are listening, but inside you are compiling a list of the other person's shortcomings and disqualifications that you are about to share. Or, at least you're entertaining such thoughts as the feedback giver goes on and on.

Even as a champion of coachability, I admit that these two inner voices show up when I hear feedback. It may be hardwired into our brain to push back. Is that pushback the right response, though? The problem is that, as the person is chattering away, I'm missing the message—perhaps something of value that might indeed be a gift. What helps is to break your *respond* action into two parts: first, capture the message; second, assess the accuracy of the input and the credentials of the giver.

But expect messy. Despite all the blogs, articles, and search results on delivering feedback effectively, the feedback giver most likely will be unskilled and nervous. (Thank goodness no one can read your mind and tap into that inner chatter.) So expect messy, clumsy, and imperfect. Your job is to quickly shift from inner-voice chatter to seeking the main message, searching for the signals. Researchers have found that establishing a routine helps quiet the negative emotions when receiving feedback. But first, you need something to help make that shift from listening to the inner-voice chatter to being receptive, curious, and open.

Mike, a supply chain director in a large retail firm, recognized a shift was in order. While debriefing his low scores on his coachability assessment, he shared:

"I realize I haven't been receiving much regular feedback since my military days, and when it does show up, now I get too emotional," he said. "I do value improving and need a better response."

I suggested he consider taking up acting.

Start Acting

During a graduate class on coachability, a student volunteered that responding to feedback well is akin to actors taking notes from the director. I had no idea what she was suggesting, so I asked her to tell me more.

She explained that early in the career of a stage actor—whether professionally or in community theater—actors are trained to "take a note." She said that at the end of every rehearsal, the play's director will give actors feedback. Called a *note*, it's critical for actors to learn to respond to a note. Learning to take a note well is regarded as the first note for a budding actor.

Curious about this "note taking," I reached out to several theater friends about acting and the coachability dimension of director feedback. Scott Eck is one such friend. A New York–based actor and CEO of Leadership Masters, a theater-based training company, Scott expected and welcomed notes with every rehearsal and performance in his career. It gave him a new perspective on how his lines and body language are being received, how his acting fits within the scene, and ways to improve. Scott told me he was always disappointed when the director didn't have a note for him.

He said, "I never saw it as criticism, but a way to be better, to have a stronger connection to the play and the audience. Without a note, I felt like I didn't have the opportunity to try something new and expand the world of the character."

Scott later passed along an adaptation of the description of actor note-taking from the Actors' Equity Association code of conduct:

ACTOR NOTES
When the director gives you notes, pay attention, and write them down. Respond to the note with a "thank you." If you need clarity, ask for greater detail, but do not argue with the note. Actors are responsible for taking the notes given to them and incorporating them into the work. Notes aren't just for you; everyone gets them. You can strengthen your own work by listening carefully to the notes given by other actors. Continually review your notes and be sure to incorporate them into your work. If you need to discuss a note, talk to the director in private.

I thought this was good advice for leaders working on their respond coachability practice. The trick to shift the mindset of inner-voice defensiveness and becoming open is to replace *feedback* with *taking a note*. Consider adopting the coachable leader professional code as:

LEADER NOTES

When someone gives you feedback, regard it as a note. Pay attention and write it down. Respond to the note with a "thank you." If you need clarity, ask for greater detail, but do not argue with the note (or listen to those defensive inner voices).

Leaders are responsible for taking the notes given to them and incorporating them into the work of leadership. Notes aren't just for you; everyone needs them. You can strengthen your leadership by listening carefully to notes, continually reviewing, and applying them as appropriate into your work. If you need to discuss a note, talk to the note giver in private.

When I am triggered to feel defensive, I've found it helpful to shift to being coachable by telling myself:

"I am just taking a note," or

"Here comes my tip of the day," or

"Hmmm, that's interesting. I'm curious."

This reminder puts me back in my coachable learning zone. It shuts down the inner voices and helps me hear the whole message. What might be your phrase to help you shift from defensive to open and curious?

Four Steps to Taking a Leader Note

t takes a bit of practice, as it does for the budding actor, to build up the routine and muscle memory of taking a note. Break it down into four steps:

Four Steps to Taking a Leader Note

1. Shift to Curious
2. Ask for Specifics and Examples
3. Paraphrase
4. "Thanks" and Next

Step One: Shift to Curious

Your first step as a coachable leader responding to feedback is shifting your mind from defensive to curious. Put off the judgment for the moment and recognize that your job is to listen and capture the message for later evaluation. Replace the defensive voices in your head with a phrase that will shift your mindset to curious and open, such as *"I'm taking a note."*

Step Two: Ask for Specifics and Examples

Think of someone you know who is a great listener. How would you describe that person? Does their body language signal full attention to what you are saying? Do they listen quietly without interrupting or dismissing you? Of course. But great listeners are more than likely to be actively engaged rather than just being quiet. They encourage you with head-nods and might even be taking notes. They ask questions—not to argue or push back, though those nasty inner voices might like that. They ask questions to understand. Remember the earlier point? Receivers should expect feedback to be messy; the giver is likely nervous and probably not well trained in the art of giving a clear message. Your role after shifting to curious is to play facilitator. Coachable leaders respond with strong listening routines that include having a ready set of follow-up questions. Consider adding a few of these to your response routine:

"That's interesting. Can you please tell me more?"

"To help me understand fully, can you provide some examples or specifics?"

"Moving forward, what might I start [or stop] doing to be more effective?"

Step Three: Paraphrase

At the end of the conversation, repeat what you've heard and understood in your own words. By paraphrasing, it allows you to confirm your understanding of what probably was a messy message. It provides confidence to the giver that you respect and value them, regardless of the message. Moreover, it signals that you're open to input in the future. At this stage, though, it's essential to recognize that you may or may not agree with the message. You are simply acknowledging what you've heard.

Step Four: "Thanks" and Next

Giving feedback is a risky act, so show a bit of appreciation for the effort with a simple *"thank you."* This step may take practice, especially if the message is hard to hear. Most times, it's appropriate to let the other person know you value their perspective and wish to think about what was said. Provide a way or time you will get back to them, such as *"Let me reflect on this for a day, and I'll get back to you."* As a coachable leader, you listen well and respond appropriately. But that doesn't mean you have to follow all of what is suggested.

There is one exception to the pause-to-reflect response. When you immediately know you are wrong and made a mistake that negatively affected someone, the correct response is to apologize immediately and make a commitment to act differently. No need to pause, reflect, and get back to anyone in this case, unless multiple people may need an apology. Part of being a highly coachable leader is recognizing when you are wrong and making amends right away.

The Chief Learning Officer Needs Coaching

had the good fortune while in my Chief Learning Officer role to be surrounded by a talented and confident staff who kept me in my learning zone. Their coaching would often show up at the end of our scheduled one-on-one meetings. They knew I would conclude the session by asking if there was anything I could do differently. One day, I learned about the chaos I had created.

Rick informed me that I was confusing the team. I had to quickly quiet my inner voice of *"You don't understand"* and shift to prepare to take a note (Step One).

"Oh, I'm sorry. Please explain what's going on," was my reply (Step Two). Rick described the mess I created by delegating the

same assignment to two employees. I had mistakenly given Rick and Becca the same project to pull together the department budget plan. This was a time-consuming task, and they were starting to bump into each other as they worked with our finance specialist. My first reaction was to defensively explain my delegation blunder was an intentional strategy, but that wasn't the case. When Rick was done painting the picture of confusion and frustration, I summarize what I had heard (Step Three).

After a pause, I admitted it was sloppy on my part. I thanked Rick and offered to schedule another meeting with him and Becca later in the day to straighten things out (Step Four).

As Rick left, I felt a mixture of embarrassment at my mistake, relief to hear about it directly, and bewilderment on how I messed up in the first place. My tip that day was to be more careful when planning assignments and keep asking for notes.

A Practice of Note Taking

The truth is our experience of receiving the so-called gift of feedback is not all that pleasant. It often comes across as critical and painful. It feels threatening to our self-esteem and most likely triggers negative emotions and defensiveness. The inner voices of *"You don't understand"* and *"Who are you"* march in to protect us. The faulty assumptions get kick-started.

Yet, coachable leaders practice getting into the learning zone of understanding the message before judging it. They train themselves to respond well. They recognize that the gift of feedback is often messy and poorly wrapped, buried beneath too much colored tissue. It requires some effort to find the value in this gift. Start by reframing incoming messages as notes to improve as actors do.

Shift to curious and open by designating a gear-switching phrase, such as *"Here comes a note."* Ask questions to clarify the message. Check for understanding by paraphrasing back what you've heard and thank the giver. Having a note-taking routine will help your coachability practice and keep you on Santa's "nice, not naughty" list of leaders.

PAUSE AND TAKE NOTE

Speaking of *notes*, you are encouraged now to take your end-of-chapter pause and return to your Coachability Notebook to capture a few thoughts. What from this chapter made the biggest impression? Write down your answers to the "2 Questions" from the following 3-2-1 Summary. Use the two exercise worksheets that follow to explore your *respond* tendencies and map out responses and practice opportunities.

Chapter Five: **RESPOND**
3-2-1 SUMMARY

3 Key Points:

1. Let's be real: feedback often feels like less of a gift and more of a threat. Our natural defenses kick in, creating too much noise on the inside to capture any value of the feedback message.

2. *Work* to quiet the internal defensive voices, such as *"You don't understand"* and *"Who are you?"*

3. Consider reframing messy feedback as just taking a note as actors are trained to do.

2 Questions:

1. What are some of my automatic, defensive voices that prevent me from fully taking in and understanding feedback from others?

2. What cue or shifting phrase can I use to quiet the defensive inner voices triggered by messy feedback and get into an actor's note-taking mindset to understand the message?

1 Next Step:

Create a practices routine to increase your ability to get into an open and curious mindset when feedback is given. Use the **Patterns and Guidelines** and **Taking Notes Practice** worksheets that follow and add to your Coachability Notebook.

Coachability Notebook: RESPOND

Patterns and Guidelines

High performers in a variety of professions use repeated practice to build "muscle memory." This preparation enables them to respond in the best way possible in stressful situations automatically. The keys are clarity on the desired response, awareness of any situational challenge, and the repeated practice of a simple routine. The same can be applied to improving your response to feedback. Whether it's a result of seeking it or not, have a practiced *response* ready.

Detecting Patterns

It's useful to start by reflecting on your past experiences and tendencies when others have given you feedback and improvement input. Complete the following worksheet to detect patterns:

Situation	Description	Key Themes and Observations
Positive: Think of a time or two when you improved based on feedback and input from others. What was the situation? What did you do, and they do that helped?		
Negative: Think of a time or two when you did not respond well to feedback and input from others. What did you do, and they do that hindered?		

General Guidelines:

Based on the above reflections, list three personal guidelines you can use to respond positively to feedback and input.

When I receive feedback and improvement notes, I will:

1. _____
   _____

2. _____
   _____

3. _____
   _____

Taking Notes Practice

In the coming two weeks, identify low-risk opportunities where you can practice taking a note (i.e., receiving feedback) as a way of building positive muscle memory. Refer to Chapter Three's seek worksheet, "Topic, Source, and Approach," for ideas.

When reflecting on each practice, describe what you did well and what you could do differently next time, including:

- Mindset of openness (being in the learning zone) vs defensive?
- Body language attentive vs distracted?
- Listening level fully present vs preoccupied (thinking of what to say next)?
- Use of questions and asking for examples vs argumentative?
- Use of paraphrasing to confirm understanding?
- Ending the conversation positively with gratitude and commitment to reflect vs an abrupt ending?
- Then identify where you can continue to take notes to keep strengthening your *response* habit.

Practice Situation:	The Approach (how you will do it):	Post-practice notes on what you did well and will do differently next time:

Next Opportunities to Practice:

CHAPTER SIX

REFLECT:
More Than You Think

Call Medical!

thought Rafael was having a stroke.

Having arrived early for a scheduled meeting, I was standing outside his office and saw something alarming. Originally looking forward to a session with a senior executive about a new leadership program, my visit suddenly turned to panic as I peered inside his office window. I expected a whirlwind of activity and executive-level productivity, perhaps a team debate around a conference table, an animated one-on-one discussion, or at least Rafael chatting on the phone or madly typing away at a computer.

But none of that was going on in his office. He was sitting there alone, pulled away from his desk, elbows on his knees, gazing ahead without focus. His administrative assistant, Dani, read my worried face and chuckled,

"Calm down, that's Rafael. He's just thinking."

"He's just thinking"—something modern leaders are rarely seen

doing, yet they are expected to. And we all have plenty to do now-adays. Yet, charging ahead full speed one hundred percent of the time has a cost. My leadership derailment study points out that such costs gives rise to emerging blind spots, poor decision-making, bad acting, and possibly career failure. I recall conducting a postmortem with the boss of a recently fired leader. When reviewing the terminated leader's misbehavior and missed signals to improve, all we could say was,

"What was she thinking?"

Most likely, she wasn't thinking enough.

More Than You Think, but Not Too Much

So how do coachable leaders devote sufficient think-time and focus to feedback notes? Reflection time is essential. Research has found that receiving feedback without reflection doesn't guarantee positive results, which sometimes makes things worse! Most of us aren't in a solid habit of reflection to begin with, and dealing with feedback can be a tricky, messy matter. Having a simple process to guide us can be invaluable in grasping the essence and value of an improvement message rather than superficially skimming over it or dragging ourselves so deep we suffer from analysis paralysis. I recall two very different coaching sessions where careful reflection uncovered the right message.

Engineer Alex was spending way too much time on his feedback report. The clear message was that people found him argumentative and a poor listener. Yet Alex didn't pick up on the key themes; he was buried in the details, having created a three-tab spreadsheet of various inputs, and was trying to create a complex model to "solve the problem." In short, he was lost in the analysis and was in danger of exhausting himself from the unnecessary, overly detailed examination with little energy left over for action.

If Alex was thinking too much, Serge in the Sales Operations was thinking too little about his report. He admitted glancing over it once and then filing it away. When asked whether there was something of value in it, he responded, *"Maybe one comment was interesting, but in general it was what I expected."* A more considered read would have helped Serge uncover a blind spot about his decision-making style that signaled trouble ahead.

One approach to help find the right balance in reflection is to follow a simple checklist. The use of checklists to aid performance was highlighted in the 2009 bestseller *The Checklist Manifesto* by Atul Gawande. The author cites numerous professions, from aviation to medical to construction, where using a simple checklist helps avoid costly and sometimes deadly errors. Whether building a skyscraper or buying recipe ingredients, Gawande warns that if you miss just one key thing, you might as well not have made the effort.

A Simple Three-Step Reflection Checklist

When reflecting on feedback and improvement notes, here's a three-step checklist to use:

What did I hear? ►	What do I think? ►	What's next?

While it's important to visit each part during the reflection process, the amount of time and intensity can vary depending on the nature of the input. For example, a simple improvement suggestion from a work colleague might need only a bit of consideration as you think through the three steps. A longer conversation with someone significant to you or a comprehensive feedback report may require more effort and reflection on your part.

What Did I Hear?

Start by reviewing what you received—from a conversation or a report such as a 360 evaluation or other assessment. Objectively capture the highlights, key points, and other items that caught your attention. The task here is not to judge the input; simply note the whole message. It's best to write it down in a journal or worksheet (or your Coachability Notebook). Doing this first helps remove some of the emotion and defensiveness that may surface and cause you to miss the message.

Questions to consider:

- *What were the key points shared?*
  Note the main points and highlights covered by the feedback.

- *What specifics were offered that helped explain things?*
  Note any examples or specifics that stood out as helpful in understanding the message. This could be what to stop or start doing.

- *What else?*
  Beyond the main message, capture what else is worth considering further.

What Do I Think?

Once you objectively capture what you heard (or read), now it's time to judge it critically. This could be briefly reflecting on the message or a more intensive analysis before considering how to act. *Not everything you receive needs to be accepted or acted upon, but it should always be reviewed.*

Consider working through the questions that match your learning style. Journal responses to these questions if you are more of an introvert. Discuss these questions with a mentor or trusted advisor if you are more of an extrovert.

Questions to consider:

- *Is this message clear or do I need more to understand it?*
  Be careful to avoid analysis paralysis, but also check for complete understanding. You may need to go back to the person to ask questions for clarity.
- *Is the input valid and credible?*
  Is the feedback coming from an informed, objective point of view, or might it be cautiously considered or even dismissed? Presume positive intent and not some hidden agenda. In some cases, you may consider checking with others on the issue, such as your truth-teller, mentor, or even an external coach or other sounding board.
- *Have I heard this before?*
  Does this feedback sound familiar or does it connect with other input you've received before? Can you detect a theme or pattern of behavior?
- *Am I sufficiently motivated to do something different?*
  Not every good idea for improvement needs to be acted upon immediately. You probably will be able to meaningfully act to improve only in one or two areas at a time. Consider: What might be the consequences of not changing right now? Or will the change require an easy shift or significant investment of time and energy? Is this something I've heard before but now matters more now?

What's Next?

There are three possible conclusions after completing "What do I think?": dismiss it, ponder it, act on it.

Dismiss it: Insufficient value or motivation may cause you to dismiss the feedback but staying open to future input is essential as a coachable leader. As a follow-up step, consider touching base with the feedback giver (from a discussion) or survey raters (if a 360) to offer appreciation for the message. It's way to say "thank you" with respect.

Ponder it: Some feedback shouldn't be dismissed, but you aren't quite sure what to do with it. Consider starting a "keep an eye out" list or journal entry on the topic for future reference. Once you become aware of a possible concern or opportunity, this may enhance your sensitivity or broaden your self-awareness. As with the "dismiss" option, making sure you "close the loop" with the feedback giver, offering something like, *"I appreciate your input, thank you. I've reflected on it and will keep it in mind moving forward."*

Act on it: This is the decision to devote time and energy to do something differently. It may be a commitment to stop doing something that negatively impacts others or start a new, positive routine. But heartfelt intention versus successful change are two different things. Highly coachable leaders are known for following through and sustaining improvements. You'll learn many of their strategies in the final *act* chapter.

A Low-Trust Dilemma Solved

Without adequate reflection, Mark was about to act on the wrong thing. During a coaching session with this middle-manager, he shared troublingly low trust ratings on his 360 report. Many would consider this the death knell of leadership. You can be smart, strategic, and energetic, but if people don't trust you, they won't follow you or give their best. Mark was about to launch a flurry of trust-building activities when we met. I was surprised at the low trust scores as I would consider him quite trustworthy.

Our conversation turned to a recently completed personality assessment where Mark scored high on innovation, seeking new ideas and experiences, and low on valuing process discipline and planning. One of the items in the personality assessment caught his attention:

"May not follow through well; gets bored quickly and moves on before completing the task."

Mark admitted that description fit him well. Digging deeper into his 360 report, follow-through on commitment was a low scoring trust question. But he scored higher on the honesty questions. Linking the two reports, he realized his lack of follow-through was the root cause. Rather than promoting his integrity and honesty, he took a different approach based on the value of stepping back and looking for connections before acting.

Mark resolved to work ahead of deadlines, regularly review his current commitments before chasing anything new, and communicate the status of his work more transparently. He was encouraged by higher scores in a subsequent survey. Mark's experience is a reminder that often there is more to the story, and not to trust jumping to action without reflection.

The Case for a Reflection Routine

n the opening story, Rafael was known as someone who took time to think and reflect. It might not have always been about feedback; it was more of a habit he'd cultivated to help him be an effective leader. Research points to the value of adopting such a habit to improve your leadership—for reflecting on feedback and beyond. Leaders who routinely reflected were found to have higher energy levels, work engagement, and influence.

In the hyperactive mode that leaders today operate in, reflection time seems to fall to the bottom of the to-do list. From emails to phone calls to catching up on what was due yesterday, it seems everything else is more urgent. Yet, consider your peak performance times in your life, the times where you were at your best. You most likely will recall many occasions where you were thoughtful, prepared, and ready. In other words, you prepared by taking time to step out of the fray and *reflect*.

As author Saul Alinsky pointed out in his classic *Rules for Radicals*,

> "Most people do not accumulate a body of experience. Most people go through a series of happenings which pass through their systems undigested. Happenings become experiences when they are digested, when they are reflected upon, related to general patterns and synthesized."

Chris Argyris, the late Harvard Business School professor and author, would add that most leaders are not very good at learning as well.

> "The focus is only on external problems to be solved and not looking inwardly where they need to reflect critically on their own behaviors, identify ways they inadvertently contribute to the organization's problems and change their way of acting."

He further argues that the very way we define and solve problems can be a source of problems in their own right. Simply put, reflecting makes it easier for new learning to come in versus sustaining old routines and mindsets.

> Reflecting is the habit of lifelong learners—
> those who have mastered living in their coach-
> able learning zone.

Nigel's Three Calendar Appointments

So how do you start digesting your experiences better and increase your learning effectiveness? Nigel Paine, author, consultant, and former BBC executive, provides a simple formula for leaders who want to build a stronger *reflect* routine. Nigel urges leaders to add three things to their calendar:

- **Reflect five minutes each day.** This time could be at the start of the day, bringing to mind your intentions of showing up as a leader this day, reviewing your scheduled meetings ahead, and planning other actions you will take that day. Or take five at the end of the day, before you "close the books" on the day, reflecting on what you did well, what you learned, and any intentions for the next day.

- **Reflect fifteen minutes a week.** As with the daily check-in, this reflection time can be scheduled at the beginning or end of the week. It's a chance to review the highlights (and perhaps lowlights) of the week, the progress on any personal development plan or focus areas, and the lessons learned. Using a journal to jot down your thoughts can help you review and conclude with forward-looking intentions for the week ahead.

- **Reflect one hour every month/quarter.** The daily and weekly reflection appointments are regular-yet-brief pauses. Some topics such as reviewing goals, improvement opportunities, or complex challenges require more time. The one-hour appointment is a chance to look more broadly at what's going on, think more deeply about what it means, and set new intentions, goals, and focal points moving forward. Use a simple agenda or checklist to guide you. Review any journal entries from the daily or weekly reflections. For introverts, this regular reflection reservation is likely a table for one. For extroverts, invite a friend or trusted advisor to join you for a discussion.

Bullet-Journaling, Strolling, and Drive-Time Reflecting

The three-appointment strategy is one of a variety of reflection routines. Find an approach that works best for you and stick with it. I've observed a few different ways leaders increased their pause routine. Ken, for example, isn't a natural writer but is in the habit of making daily entries in his "decision bullet journal." He captures decisions made and thoughts about his decision process in a notebook. The entries are typically short, but over time the daily notes help him improve his decision-making and his problem-solving approach.

Joining a new organization or starting a new project can be an ideal time to start a "situation journal." Upon promotion to a new field operations role, Maya noted daily encounters for the first ninety days. Her entries were prodded by three simple questions:

- Who did I meet?
- What did I hear?
- Are there any implications for me?

A more active reflection routine is adding a daily stroll or exercise break to mull over reflection questions. You could combine the two, strolling while reflecting, and then do your situational journaling upon return. But I wouldn't recommend writing while driving.

Janice steered her thinking with a drive-time reflection technique. As a manufacturing plant manager, she dedicated her ride at the start of her day—sans news radio or podcasts—to contemplate her leadership intentions that day. Her drive home was time to review what transpired and her actions. Once on her trip home she started ruminating over an unnecessarily stressful encounter with her second-shift supervisors. Rather than stew on the problem overnight, she turned the car around and went back to the plant to apologize to the team. The return visit was well received, and Janice continues to use drive time as her reflection time.

Got a Minute? or a Few More?

Highly coachable leaders take time to reflect—to adequately consider any notes received or just as a general think-time routine for ongoing learning. Even a minute or two can make a difference, and a few more can elevate your coachability in significant ways.

"The ability to maintain perspective in the midst of action is critical," advise authors Ron Heifetz and Marty Linsky. "You have to get off the dance floor and move up to the balcony . . . and ask 'what's really going on here.'" Rafael's balcony was his office thinking pose—elbows on knees, pulled away from this desk, gazing off in the distance. Janice used her commute time. Ken and Maya used journaling. Regular reflection helped each of them gain a fresh perspective on the action, what was going on, and what steps to take back on the dance floor of leadership. Find your reflection balcony and visit it often.

PAUSE AND TAKE NOTE

If you've been pausing after every chapter to write key ideas and thoughts in your Coachability Notebook, you are well on your way to improving your reflect routine. And you know what's coming next: a reminder to jot down ideas from this chapter and respond to the "3-2-1" questions. Two of the worksheets that follow will guide you as you think about feedback. Use the journaling worksheet to help you start or expand your overall reflection practice.

Chapter Six: **REFLECT**
3-2-1 SUMMARY

3 Key Points:

1. Set aside time after you receive feedback and improvement notes to fully digest the message and consider the value of acting upon it.

2. Use a simple checklist to guide your feedback reflection: What did I hear? What do I think? What's next?

3. Make a regular appointment to build a reflection routine with five minutes daily, fifteen minutes weekly, and one-hour monthly sessions.

2 Questions:

1. What questions would help me reflect on the full value of any feedback or note to improve?

2. What type of reflection habit best fits my personality: quiet journaling and think-time or regular conversations with a mentor and trusted advisor?

1 Next Step:

For one week, start or end your day by journaling. (Refer to the following Coachability Notebook worksheet, **Reflection Journaling.**)

Coachability Notebook: REFLECT

Hear-Think-Decide

Here is a process to reflect on feedback and improvement input. Respond to each question to guide your thinking and capture the key insights and value. You can also use these questions with a coach or trusted advisor for a discussion about the feedback as well. Often returning to review your notes a day later can provide a fresh perspective.

Steps and Questions to Consider	My Notes:
What Did I Hear?	
1. What were the main points and overarching themes?	
2. What were the details, specifics, and examples?	
What Do I Think?	
3. What was unclear that I might need to follow up about?	
4. To what degree was the input valid and credible? Was there any aspect of value before I might dismiss it?	

5. How does this information connect with other feedback I've received before or other thoughts I've had? Does anything point to a potential blind spot I need to explore further?	
6. Is there any part of the message that I should reach out to a trusted advisor, mentor, or truth-teller for their perspective?	
7. To what degree am I motivated to act? What are the benefits of acting? What are the risks if I don't?	

What's Next?

8. How will I thank those giving me feedback and let them know I have considered it (and any necessary actions)?	
9a. **Dismiss:** What part of the feedback might I dismiss and why? Is there at least an incorrect perception out there I need to address?	
9b. **Ponder:** What do I need to think more about, and how I will keep track of the feedback topic?	
9c. **Act:** What might be my initial steps based on the feedback? What would "success" look like? What additional support or resources should I find to help initiate and sustain improvement effort?	

Decision Action Plan:

10. What have I decided to do based on this reflection?	

Digesting a 360 in Five Easy Steps

A common tool for greater self-awareness and development is called a 360-degree survey. This is where those surrounding a leader, such as a manager, peers, and employees, provide feedback on behaviors and suggestions for improvement. What is uncommon is the reflection necessary to make the most out of a report.

First, let's face the fact that it's an emotional roller coaster to read how others have ranked you and what they've commented on. The acronym S.A.R.A.H. is a fitting description of the ups and downs of the emotional read—starting with Shock (Oh, look at that low score/nasty comment!), Anger (How dare they say that!), Rejection (That's just plain wrong!), Acceptance (Well, maybe there's some truth here) and Hope (I think I can work on that).

Second, unless you have a planned approach, you probably are stuck somewhere in the S.A.R. (Shock, Anger, Rejection) part of the ride. Here's a five-step approach you can use to make the ride of a 360 worth the trip.

One: First Reading—	**Date of 1st Read and Reaction Notes:**
Read it over with then put it aside.	
Read it but don't do anything yet—no flaming emails, no nasty calls or conversations, and certainly no jumping off cliffs. We are drawn to the low scores and critical comments. We usually gravitate to dwelling on weaknesses and low scores during the first reading as skip over the positive items.	
Then: Pause—perhaps set it aside for a day. Get a good night's sleep.	
Things will make more sense the next morning.	

Two: Second Reading—	**Date of 2nd Read and Notes:**
Usually, the second reading provides a more complete perspective and helps you catch ideas you missed on the first pass. As you re-read, take notes in three columns: positives, negatives, unsure. Don't overanalyze, don't dismiss, just notice and write.	**Positives:**
	Negatives:
	Unsure:

Three: Check-in Chat—	Check-in Chat Partner and Date of Chat:
Next, plan a check-in conversation with a trusted advisor, coach, or friend. Stay open and curious as you share the report and your thoughts.	
Use a simple template to summarize your notes to guide your conversation, such as: What are the 3–5 strength themes? What are the 1–2 most interesting development or improvement themes? What are some questions now or areas of interest to explore or consider?	**Key questions for conversation:**

Four: Third and Final Reading—	Notes and insights from the conversation:
After your check-in session, it's time to decide your actions. What to keep in mind? What to work on, or explore?	**My Actions:** **—Keep in mind:**
	—To leverage or work on:
	—Needs further exploration:
Five: Save the Insight and Throw the Report Away – Keep your notes but close out the report. The 360 is a snapshot and you are a movie. Time to take considered action and follow up. Time to move on!	

Reflection Journaling

Reflection writing or journaling is a useful technique to achieve new levels of creativity and critical thinking. It is the step-back-and-pause that can help you in the middle of busy days, stay focused, and handle difficult challenges and the emotions that can go with them.

Log five to ten minutes of journaling on a daily or weekly basis. Some leaders find an early-morning routine helpful to start the day with the right mindset, and others use writing in the evening to clear their minds of the day's stressors. Consider starting with a set of standard questions to begin the process and then refine the questions over time. Of course, feel free to go beyond the questions to write down what's on your mind and feeling.

Sample questions:

- What did I intend to do today? Where was my focus today? What did I ignore or miss?
- What worked well? What didn't work well?
- To what degree did I operate in my coachable learning zone? What helped and what hindered?
- What helped my effectiveness, and what got in the way?
- What observations and lessons learned can I take from my experiences today?
- How did I treat others today? In what way did I create energy and inspire motivation?
- How well did I listen to others?
- In what way did I provide coaching to my team?
- How did I make progress on my personal goals?
- How could I apply today's lessons to be better tomorrow?

Another approach to journaling is using a bullet-list method to quickly capture thoughts in general or with a particular focus. For example, a decision bullet journal to capture ideas on what decisions you made today or are thinking about making soon. Another theme could be around people and interesting encounters you've had that day or week (e.g., Whom did you meet? What were the topics or interesting points? Any implications for you moving forward?). The value of the bullet-journal approach is it's a quick and easy way to get in the habit of writing a bit and slowing down to reflect. Look back on your entries from time to time to detect patterns or insights.

CHAPTER SEVEN:

ACT:
An Experiment of One

Getting Back on Track

"I work late every night, leave exhausted, and then wake up in the middle of the night thinking of what to add to my to-do list. I know things need to change, but I feel stuck."

My former executive MBA student Kory was recounting her frustrations as a recently promoted project leader. We would connect at a coffee shop for catching up and coaching from time to time. Her initial enthusiasm at taking over a big software installation was fading fast as the project was now three months behind schedule, over budget, and under a demoralized project team. In recounting recent feedback notes, Kory was falling back into old habits of doing all the work herself, then not having time to plan or consult with department leaders. To get the project back on track and Kory back to a good night's sleep would require a new strategy. She hoped to hear how coachable leaders move from reflection to action successfully.

At this stage of becoming a more coachable leader, you've affirmed the value of feedback and seeking improvement ideas. Check. You've taken the brief coachability self-assessment. Check. You've solicited input skillfully from others and listened openly. Check. You've followed the reflection steps. Check. And now it's time to act.

Kory needed to act quickly to get herself and the software project back on track. Over coffee, I shared what highly coachable leaders do to manage personal change successfully: they know the odds of change and reset the balance in their favor. As you move to action, check your change balance.

Rebalancing the Odds Against

Highly coachable leaders begin by thinking of failure. They anticipate potential obstacles ahead and design strategies to prevent them. They plan how to recover when they trip up or stall out. Recent personal change studies support the idea of considering what could go wrong, particularly identifying what things have tripped you up before. Kory was surprised that we began crafting her improvement plan by contemplating failure but started to see where the common "odds against" would push her off track.

Odds Against Change

Driving Without a Destination (Unclear)
Someone Else's Idea (Uninspired)
Why Did I Walk Into This Room? (Distracted)
Olympic Dreams With
Couch Potato Habits (Unrealistic)
Fuzzy Math (Missing Factor)

Driving Without a Destination (Unclear)

Kory's desire to turn around low team morale was a fuzzy notion that she needed to lead differently. She heard the message from her employees, but she didn't see a clear direction to take. Being better or trying harder was about all she could see. Having broad intentions to change without a well-defined picture of success leads to more wandering than improving. Our urge to prematurely act without thoughtful consideration provides temporary satisfaction of progress. But it could lead to a dead end.

Someone Else's Idea (Uninspired)

Even if headed in a clear-cut direction, improvement efforts can stall before arriving at the destination. An external message or signal may jump-start action, but internal fuel is indispensable. Feeling obligated to act without internal commitment may generate temporary compliance, but it rarely produces sustained or meaningful change. I could sense this wasn't going to trip up Kory. She linked the signals of the project slipping and the team's notes of dissatisfaction with her desire to succeed as an empowering project leader.

Why Did I Walk Into This Room? (Distracted)

While motivated on the inside, the outside distraction of her project in chaos proved to be a bigger challenge. The lack of sleep didn't help either. Our scheduled coffee check-in served as Kory's wake-up call to refocus and regain momentum. As leaders, our lives are busy and demanding. We are easily distracted by the crisis of the moment, the demands of the day. At times we can completely lose track of our development. Much like having too much on your mind, you catch yourself not knowing why you walked into a room. (Was it to let the dog out or retrieve your reading glasses?) You may be in the right room for improvement but have forgotten what you were supposed to do differently.

Olympic Dreams with Couch Potato Habits (Unrealistic)

Sometimes we stuff the improvement room with a bulky and complex action plan. We overcommit to Olympic-size training schedules but are held back with couch potato habits. Kory was in the early planning stages, so this wasn't a major risk. Yet, for many of us, we internalize the improvement notes we hear, reflect on the value, and produce an over-the-top transformation plan. Over time, the sheer size of the "new me" becomes a burden to exercise in our daily lives. Without having simple, doable starting points, the big, complex improvement campaign can even repel us from trying anything. We give up and stay on the couch.

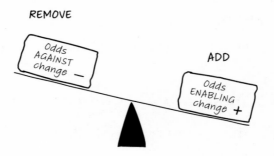

Rebalance change efforts by removing the odds against and loading up the odds of success enablers.

Fuzzy Math (Missing Factor)

A coffee shop napkin became my teaching "whiteboard" as I drew up a four-factor change formula for Kory. Each factor is essential and has a multiplier effect on the overall calculation of success. In other words, you can get three of the four factors right and still produce a zero result without the fourth one.

Successful Change =

Accurate Awareness of What to Change X
Sufficient Motivation and Self-Image X
Applicable Knowledge, Skills, Tools X
Sustained Effort

This missing-factor calculation equates to fuzzy math by:

- Jumping to a faulty diagnosis
- Complying without commitment and not seeing ourselves as succeeding
- Lacking relevant resources (knowledge, skills, tools)
- Falling back to old, comfortable ways

Kory realized her current self-image would limit her success. Being action-oriented was her brand, but now that was working against her job to lead more than do. Her heroic "jump in and save the day" felt comfortable but stunted her team's capabilities to solve their problems. Defaulting to her comfort zone and not her learning zone kept her from her leader job: to better coordinate workflows, manage scope-creep, and influence stakeholder expectations. To strengthen her change formula, she needed to redefine her self-image and brand as a project team leader rather than a save-the-day firefighter. She also recognized a gap in her planning capabilities, with her role requiring a robust set of project management tools to rebalance the change-odds in her favor.

Rebalancing Odds in Our Favor

A long with anticipating what could go wrong, coachable leaders load up what will help things go right. These change enablers rebalance the odds in their favor. I reviewed their best practices with Kory and sprinkled in recent personal change research as we looked for the best ways to build up her odds of success.

Odds in Favor of Change Enablers

Flip the Odds-Against Traps (Lighten Up)
Try Small Steps First (Experiment)
Park Downhill (Surround Support)
Add Reminders and Nudges (Choose Well)
Go for Five (Load Up Activators)
Cue Sustained Success (Habit Building)
Set a Daily Dashboard (Check-in Questions)

Flip the Odds-Against Traps (Lighten Up)

Lightening up the weight of "odds-against traps" will rebalance change in your favor. Flip the negative odds-against traps into positive enablers. Construct a clear picture of what success looks like. Affirm your personally motivating "why" to improve. Use reminders to blend your action plan into your everyday routines. Check to ensure your plan is sufficient to make a difference and simple enough to apply. Hold an image of your success in mind while recognizing that sustained improvement is often uneven, and forward progress is living in the coachable learning zone with adjustments and pivots.

Kory created a delegation notebook and used the first page to spell out her aspirational "leadership brand" as a strategic planner, influential change agent, and skillful delegator. She recognized this was an aspirational goal, but the new self-image provided a meaningful long-term destination for her short-term efforts. Next, she wrote down the benefits of change, such as having a better work–life balance for her family and catching up on sleep. Using what's called the "heaven and hell" motivator, she listed what success and failure would produce. Seeing the contrast of the status quo "hell" and spelling out the "heaven" upside fueled her motivation to step into change more fully. For the delegation "hell," Kory noted that taking work away from her team produced employee dissatisfaction, personal burnout, and career trouble. Project "heaven" was getting the software installation back on track and opening opportunities for promotion. She set the first half hour every Friday to review her progress, lessons learned, and plans for the following week. She sought an internal mentor for weekly coaching sessions to learn more about project management planning and influencing project stakeholders.

Try Small Steps (Experiment)

Simple starts, small risks, and willingness to try something new are small steps that lead to bigger things. Coachable leaders see themselves as "an experiment of one" by trying new behaviors or routines. One step could be asking yourself, *"How can I be ten percent better about this?"* The current literature on habit-building advises starting a change effort with what's familiar, extending to small, new steps, and building momentum from there. In Kory's journey to improve delegation and trust her staff more, she started turning over small tasks to build confidence. The spirit of experimentation kept her in her coachable learning zone as she applied new planning routines and began regular stakeholder coffee hour meetings to build better relationships and support for the software project.

Park Downhill (Surround Support)

Another step to take is "park downhill." Dr. Theresa Glomb, a colleague at the University of Minnesota, explains that a car pointed in the right direction and parked downhill uses gravity to get into motion. She advocates setting up your environment to support your change, making it easier to do the things you want to do and harder to do the things you don't.

Parking your high-priority project material out at the end of your day can jump-start next morning's productivity. Removing distractions would make it harder to get off task as you start your day. Regularly connecting with a coach or mentor is another way to keep you moving in the right direction. They can surround you with the fuel of wisdom, encouragement, and accountability for your change journey.

Kory met with each employee weekly to review delegated work progress and any support needed. She added a pause before taking on any task herself and considered if a staff member could do it instead. Her regular mentoring sessions and our coffee encounters provided support to keep her moving in the right direction.

Add Reminders and Nudges (Choose Well)

Each day we face thousands of choices on what to do, and we mainly operate by default and shortcuts. Make the default choices in favor of your planned change. Recent psychology and behavioral economics research highlight the power of reminders and nudges to keep you engaged and moving forward. Place your improvement plan where you'll see it regularly. Post a copy in your office, an improvement phrase on your phone background, a weekly reminder into your online calendar. Use the "three appointments" strategy from the reflect practice chapter: hold time on your schedule to review your plan and progress by integrating into the five minutes a day/fifteen minutes a week/one hour a month reflect appointments. Kory's delegation notebook, weekly mentoring meetings, and scheduled planning sessions proved to be her best reminder routines.

Go For Five (Load Up Activators)

Loading up for success pays off when what you write down comes alive. Highly coachable leaders employ tactics I call "activators" to successfully move from intent to action. Activator examples include telling others about your plans, asking for help, and scheduling progress check-ins. My research finds the more, the better. A sample of over one hundred mid-career leaders were measured six months after completing a training course to determine if they achieved their plan and how many activators they used. The number of activators made a big difference. Leaders who implemented one hundred percent of their plans employed an average of five activation tactics. Leaders who failed to achieve half of their plans used only two activation tactics.

Other people noticed the difference. The follow-up study also polled managers, employees, and peers concerning the leader's improvement (or lack of change). The five+ activator leaders scored significantly higher across seven improvement measurements versus the two tactics leaders in such areas as:

- Increased overall leadership effectiveness.
- Noticeable improvement efforts.
- Improvement made a positive impact on the organization.

See the Activation Tactics worksheet in the Coachability Notebook section to load up on at least five approaches to support your plan.

Cue Sustained Success (Habit Building)

Getting off to a strong start is encouraging, but how do you sustain progress for the long run? Our short-term change needs to evolve to be a regular habit. Habits are a hot topic, with several bestsellers, including *The Power of Habit, Atomic Habits,* and *The Compound Effect,* collectively selling more than four million copies. As one author stated, *"Habits are the compound interest of self-improvement."*

> *Our short-term change needs to evolve to be a regular habit. You can apply the habit building approach to sustain your overall growth as a coachable leader as well.*

Think about habits in five stages:

- **Cue:** the stimulus for the habit, such as a particular situation or environment.
- **Craving:** the internal motivation triggered by the cue.
- **Response:** the behavioral response to the cue to satisfy the craving.
- **Reward:** the short-term payoff for the response.
- **Consequence:** the long-term effect of the response.

All five parts were in play as I coached Len, a divisional president. He was digesting a message that his staff regarded him as a meddling micromanager. Len was surprised as he considered himself a good leader and wondered what was going on. After a series of candid discussions with his employees, Len's micromanager habit came into focus:

- **Cue:** in staff meetings when he felt his team wasn't hearing him.
- **Craving:** Len's drive to win, get things right, and concern that his team didn't recognize risk.
- **Response:** his staff noticed that the micromanaging would begin when Len started "talking with his hands." Usually a calm person, Len's body language shift was the tell.
- **Reward:** once the hands started flailing, his staff would shut down and just nod in agreement. Len misinterpreted their acquiescence as accepting his point of view and relaxed, thinking they were now getting things right. (In reality, the staff was giving up and just doing whatever Len would dictate.)
- **Consequence:** the staff was now joking about watching out for Len and his "jazz hands." It produced cynicism and low morale.

To break the habit, Len began noticing when his hands started dancing in a staff meeting. He would consciously put his hands down, take a breath, and candidly share that he was getting uncomfortable. He would ask what the team thought they heard him say and their reaction. Over time, Len established a new habit that worked well for him and his team. While his staff occasionally reminded him to put his hands down, Len successfully sustained a positive habit and role-modeled coachability for his team.

Habit building works for stopping destructive behaviors, as Len discovered, and establishing positive ones. Make sustained improvement a habit by knowing:

- **What's the Cue?** The trigger to create a new behavior or signal that something needs to change.
- **What's the underlying Craving?** The motivation to link to a positive response or the need to replace a negative one.
- **What's the best Response?** Determine how to make the positive behavior easier to do or the negative behavior more difficult or avoidable.

- **What's the Reward?** Identify what can be satisfying and reinforcing for the right behavior and unsatisfying for the wrong behavior.
- **What's the Consequence?** See how the positive behavior reinforces your desired image of what you want to be (or see how the negative behavior results in what you don't want to be).

You can apply this approach to sustain your overall growth as a coachable leader as well. Each practice—a *seek* two-question query, a *respond* listening technique, a *reflect* appointment pause—can become second nature by habit building. Kory constructed a daily dashboard to track her new habits.

Set a Daily Dashboard (Check-in Questions)

During one coffee session, I explained to Kory how executive coach Marshall Goldsmith uses a simple routine to maintain his self-improvement efforts. At the end of every day, he answers questions linked to his values and self-improvement goals. He's up to thirty-two questions but advises his clients to start with a few. He scores his daily answers on a simple spreadsheet with a 1 (yes, I did that today) or 0 (no, I missed that today). At times, he's even paid someone to call him at the same time every night—no matter where in the world he is—and pose the questions, such as:

Did I do my best to:
- Be engaged?
- Build relationships?
- Say/do something nice for a loved one?
- Follow up with clients?

He'll log fitness goals such as hours slept, sit-ups done, and current weight. The benefits of this daily routine are numerous: the dashboard reminds you what's most important, brings a simple level of accountability (and positive recognition for progress), and makes patterns visible over time.

As a natural scorekeeper, Kory tried a version of this approach by keeping a scorecard in her delegation record where she tallied weekly what she had delegated and when she caught herself about to do what her employees should be doing. She also tracked her success in dedicating time weekly for planning and consulting with internal stakeholders. Kory also appreciated that her project manager mentor kept her accountable by reviewing her dashboard.

Better Odds and Second Acts

Kory was upbeat when we met six months later. She looked rested, confident, and even picked up the tab to celebrate getting the software installation project back on track. She admitted to losing a valuable employee during the turnaround but later found a promising replacement. Kory was making good progress navigating from DIYer to leader.

A Final Enabler: Forgiveness and Reset

All these tactics will improve your odds of success, but progress is rarely linear or guaranteed. The coachability journey is knowing that not every day will be your best, and we all fall short at times. The difference is about restorative forgiveness, recommitment, and finding hope in a second try. Coachability isn't about being perfect; it's about being willing to learn and try again.

Both Len and Kory stumbled along the way but worked to stay in their learning zone. After one misstep, Len remarked, *"I know I'm not perfect, there's always more to learn."* Throughout Kory's improvement journey, she saw that all her coachability practices were in play. She regularly sought out input and perspectives on her and delegation efforts and looked for signals of progress or problems. While challenging at times, she strengthened her *respond* practices and open-listening routines, particularly when hearing from project stakeholders on what was falling short of expectations and from her mentor on what she still had to learn. And even with a crazy-busy schedule, she ensured she made time to step out of the fray, reflect, and regain a learning perspective.

PAUSE AND TAKE NOTE—FINAL ACT

As you finish this last chapter, turn to your Coachability Notebook one more time to write any insights, answer the "2 Questions" from the 3-2-1 Summary, and then use the worksheets as templates for your action planning. Also, write down the "odds against" change factors you've experienced and the "odds in favor" enablers that have worked for you in the past. This inventory can serve as a baseline of your change tendencies.

Page through your Notebook one last time and add a summary. Use these three prompts to consolidate your thoughts and takeaways:

- The three most valuable ideas for me from this book are . . .
- If I don't do anything else as a result of this reading, I will certainly . . .
- One habit I will build to keep me in my coachable learning zone is ...

Finally, write down a reminder to retake the "Brief Coachability Self-Assessment" in six months to see how your "experiment of one," your coachability journey, is coming along.

Chapter Seven: **ACT**
3-2-1 SUMMARY

3 Key Points:

1. Personal change is about rebalancing the odds in your favor by unloading "odds against" barriers and adding "odds in favor" enablers.

2. Being unclear, unmotivated, distracted, having unrealistic plans, or lacking critical abilities are factors causing us to not follow through successfully with improvement decisions.

3. See yourself as an "experiment of one," adding support, nudges, and habit-building tactics to improve your odds of success.

2 Questions:

1. As I think about times I've succeeded at change and times I've fallen short, which enablers and barriers were present?

2. How can I use the five parts of habit-building to strengthen a current improvement effort?

1 Next Step:

Identify one negative behavior you need to manage better and how you can set up a "watch out" intention of early derailment indicators, avoidance mechanisms, and recovering tactics.
(See the Coachability Notebook worksheet **Watch Out Planner.**)

Coachability Notebook: ACT

Rebalancing-the-Odds Planner

Begin your action planning by considering what obstacles you might face and how you can use positive enablers to help you succeed.

My *Act* Improvement Objective:

Negative Odds Against Improvement	**Enabler Odds in Favor of Improvement**
Which of the following negative odds might I face when implementing this plan?	Which of the following favorable odds enablers can I employ to succeed?
☐ Driving Without a Destination (Unclear)	☐ Flip the Odds-Against Traps (Lighten Up)
☐ Someone Else's Idea (Uninspired)	☐ Try Small Steps First (Experiment)
☐ Why Did I Walk into This Room? (Distracted)	☐ Park Downhill (Surround Support)
☐ Olympic Dreams with Couch Potato Habits (Unrealistic)	☐ Add Reminders and Nudges (Choose Well)
☐ Fuzzy Math (Missing Factor)	☐ Go for Five (Load Up Activators)
☐ Other negative odds traps I've experienced before:	☐ Cue Sustained Success (Habit Building)
	☐ Set a Daily Dashboard (Check-In Questions)
	☐ Other positive odds enablers I've used before:

How I will avoid the most challenging negative odds or recover if these trip up my *act* plan:	How I will incorporate the most helpful positive odds enablers with this *act* plan:

Activation Tactics

Here is a list of tactics to help enable the *act* part of *Coachability*. A study of leaders who successfully act and sustain improvement based on feedback and coaching applied a combination of these tactics. "Communicating to others" and "Frequent reminders" were the two tactics most associated with successful implementation. Review this list and incorporate at least five of these tactics in your worksheet. Be sure to keep the worksheet visible as a reminder to you.

- [ ] Communicate your development goals and plans to others.
- [ ] Ask others for support in achieving plan goals.
- [ ] Align improvement plan actions that contribute to work objectives and responsibilities.
- [ ] Ensure improvement is personally meaningful. Write down the benefits and payoffs.
- [ ] Check the plan items, so they are practical and actionable.
- [ ] Observe others who excel at what you are trying to improve and apply what you see.
- [ ] Write down specific situations for improvement on what to start doing more and what to stop doing.
- [ ] Assemble valuable resources to achieve the plan (e.g., articles, books, online material, training, etc.).
- [ ] Build in frequent reminders and review of plan actions. Post your plan where you will see it daily.
- [ ] Schedule time to work on plan items and review progress. Do a daily check-in and a weekly review.
- [ ] Engineer ways to get reinspired and reminded of the importance of improvement.
- [ ] Establish a peer coaching partner to meet regularly to support each other.
- [ ] Seek a mentor to provide guidance, wisdom, accountability, and support.
- [ ] Periodically ask others for feedback on your action plan progress.

Activation Tactics to Apply and Specific Ways to Use Them:

Activation Tactic	How to Apply:

Watch Out Planner

Being mindful of what *not* to do and having a plan to prevent or recover is a helpful way to sustain your forward momentum and avoid derailment. Note your top two or three watch-out topics, early indicators of negative behavior, blind spots, or faulty assumptions emerging, and what you can do about it.

Example

Watch-Out Areas and Description:	Early Indicators (Example behaviors and triggers)	Preventive Measures and Recovery Responses
Too Skeptical · Impact: hurts collaboration and relationship building with peers.	**Situation/Triggers:** · When I'm not involved in decisions and don't know what is going on. · Seeing problems as win-lose. **Contributing Factors:** · Personality traits of low social and relationship-building sensitivities. · High drive to achieve and control.	**Keep Doing:** · Analyze and understand situations and motivations of others. **Stop Doing:** · Approaching world with negative, "glass-is-half-empty" attitude, especially when under stress. **Start Doing:** · More looking at positive traits of peers and situations. · Reframing the story of others as having positive intent and bringing positives to the situation. · More open-minded by asking questions and listening to understand more. · If conflict, ask if this battle is worth fighting. · Weekly reaching out and informally socializing with peers. · Track peer connections in the next 90 days.

Watch-Out Areas and Description:	Early Indicators (Example behaviors and triggers)	Preventive Measures and Recovery Responses

A Sustaining Checklist Dashboard

Use regular reminders to check progress and sustain momentum. Use the checklist log to set up a daily dashboard to track progress and maintain your effort over time. Below is a sample of daily/weekly questions to create a checklist for your review routine or for trusted advisor check-in conversation.

Sample Questions:

- Did I listen well and not interrupt others today?
- Did I stay focused on important priorities?
- Did I encourage others and avoid criticizing?

- Did I reach out today and strengthen a relationship?
- Did I take time for family and friends?
- Did I start the day with a clear focus and intent?
- Did I exercise X minutes?

- Did I make nutritious food choices?
- Did I follow up on my commitments?
- Did I take time to learn something new?
- Did I get enough rest and recovery?

Sample Checklist Log:

Review Check: Date, Yes/No	Date	Date	Date	Date	Date	Date	Date	Date	Date
Check-In Question: Did I . . .									
1.									
2.									
3.									
4.									
5.									

One Final Note

Can you recall your last **teachable moment**? You might have made a mistake, something didn't go as planned, or even something went better than expected. Someone might have helped you recognize the lesson, or maybe the power of the moment caused you to reflect on your own. These are the coachable "I'll never forget that" moments that propel us to be better.

But there are also times when the lesson is waiting, and we pass it by, much like the Warmer/Colder volunteer from the First Words. We rush ahead with our busy lives, not looking for or picking up on the signals that would help us improve. Blind spots may emerge, faulty assumptions may overtake us; our career plans could derail, or at least an uneasy feeling overtakes us that something isn't quite right.

What if you could capture more of those lessons and accelerate your growth as a more trusted and capable leader? That's the mindset and practice of being highly coachable:

- Looking for new perspectives
- Being curious when potential lessons present themselves
- Getting into the habit of stepping back to reflect
- Trying out new approaches

I hope that this book reminds you of those powerful moments in your learning zone: confident and curious, strong yet humble, open and teachable. If you'd like to learn more about coachability, please visit **www.thecoachableleader.com** for additional resources and the latest research.

Whether you are going for a transformation or simply a "ten percent better" habit, I wish you the best in applying the insights and practices you've learned here as you continue to build your leadership coachability superpower.

—*Kevin D. Wilde*

Reference Notes

First Words:

1. **Every year billions of dollars and millions of training . . .** Gurdjian, Pierre, Halbeisen, Thomas, and Lane, Kevin. "Why leadership-development programs fail." McKinsey Quarterly (January 2014). www.mckinsey.com/featured-insights/leadership/why-leadership-development-programs-fail

2. **CEOs still complain that a lack of sufficient leadership talent is a top threat . . .** Mitchell, Charles, Ray, Rebecca L., Ozyildirim, A., Maselli, Ilaria, and Peterson, Dana M. (2021). C-Suite Challenges™ 2021, Conference Board, Inc. (annual survey)
(*Note:* I've been following the annual Conference Board CEO and C-Suite survey since 1999, and lack of sufficient talent and developing the next generation of leaders are consistently ranked in the top-five concerns and business-growth limiters. So even with the billions of dollars McKinsey noted, the ROI of leadership training and coaching programs seems to be quite low.)

Chapter One:

1. **Two findings provided the most insight. . .** i4cp 2017 Conference. "Kevin Wilde on studying success through failure." YouTube video. April 7, 2017. www.youtube.com/watch?v=EYqBjbZL_fo&t=15s2.

2. **We created a coachability index and analyzed their global data set. . .** Zenger, Jack, Folkman, Joe., & Wilde, Kevin. *"How coachable are your leaders?"* Webinar. May 1, 2017. www.youtube.com/watch?v=4C0ivK1LHC8. (Note: The original coachability index was composed of three items from the Zenger-Folkman Extraordinary 360 survey: Actively looks for opportunities to get feedback to improve him/herself, makes a real effort to improve based on feedback from others, creates an atmosphere of continual improvement in which self and others push to exceed the expected results.)

3. **Another meta-study of thirty years of feedback-seeking. . .** Anseel, Frederik, Beatty, Adam S., Shen, Winny, Lievens, Filip, and Sackett,

Paul R. "How Are We Doing After 30 Years? A Meta-Analytic Review of the Antecedents and Outcomes of Feedback-Seeking Behavior." *Journal of Management*, vol. 41, no. 1, (May 2013): 318–348. https://doi.org/10.1177/0149206313484521

Chapter Two:

1. **A relook at the assessment of 50,000 leaders . . . ; The analysis found two and a half times higher levels of employee motivation. . . ; The mystery started to unravel with one more study. . .** Zenger, Jack., Folkman, Joe., & Wilde, K. "How coachable are your leaders?" Webinar. May 1, 2017. www.youtube.com/watch?v=4C0ivK1LHC8.

2. **My investigation found study after study reinforcing the power of coachability. . .** de Stobbeleir, Katleen.E., Ashford, Susan J., and Buyens, Dirk. ("Self-Regulation of Creativity at Work: The Role of Feedback-seeking Behavior in Creative Performance." Academy of Management Journal, vol. 54, no.4 (May 2011): 811–831. doi.org/10.5465/amj.2011.64870144.

   Goldberg, Walter H. "Book Reviews: Gifford Pinchot III: Intrapreneuring: Why You Don't Have to Leave the Corporation to Become an Entrepeneur 1985, New York: Harper and Row. 368 pages." *Organization Studies,* vol.7, no. 4 (October 1986): 398–399. doi.org/10.1177/017084068600700408.

   Weiss, Jake and Merrigan, Maureen. "Employee Coachability: New Insights to Increase Employee Adaptability, Performance, and Promotability in Organizations." *International Journal of Evidence Based Coaching and Mentoring,* vol.19, no. 1 (February 2021): 121–136. https://doi.org/10.24384/kfmw-ab52

3. **Coachable sales leaders produce greater sales. . .** Shannahan, Kirby L.J., Bush, Alan J., and Shannahan, Rachel J. "Are your salespeople coachable? How salesperson coachability, trait competitiveness, and transformational leadership enhance sales performance." *Journal of the Academy of Marketing Science,* vol. 41, no. 1 (January 2012): 40–54. https://doi.org/10.1007/s11747-012-0302-9

4. **Angel investors are more likely to invest in entrepreneurs who show greater levels of coachability . . .** Ciuchta, Michael P., Letwin, Chaim R., Stevenson, Regan M., and McMahon, S.R. (2015). "Betting on the coachable entrepreneur: Introduction of a new construct and scale." Academy of Management's Annual Meeting *Proceedings* conference publication. doi.org/10.5465/ambpp.2015.15065abstract

5. **Further, good things happen with a leader who has a high engaged workforce . . .** Kumar, V. & Pansari, A. "Measuring the Benefits of Employee Engagement." *MIT Sloan Management Review,* vol. 56, no. 4 (June 2015): 67–72. sloanreview.mit.edu/article/measuring-the-benefits-of-employee-engagement

6. **My favorite study compared the coaching skills of the manager vs. the coachability of the employees . . .** Weiss, Jake A., Merrigan, Maureen. (2021). "Employee Coachability: New Insights to Increase Employee Adaptability, Performance, and Promotability in Organizations." *International Journal of*

Evidence Based Coaching and Mentoring, vol. 19, no. 1 (February 2021: 121-136. https://doi.org/10.24384/kfmw-ab52

7. **Sally Grimes, CEO of Cliff Bars. . .** Gaparro, Annie. "How the CEO of Cliff Bars stays hungry." *Wall Street Journal,* January 30, 2021.

8. **A simple Google Trends search. . .** Results from Google Trends search conducted May 1, 2021.

9. **Getting outranked. . .** Amazon book ranking search results conducted June 20, 2021.

10. **A study of over 5,000 leaders who failed. . .** Leadership IQ Study: Why New Hires Fail. Cision PRWeb, September 20, 2005.

11. **$300 billion leadership training industry. . .** Westfall, Chris. "Leadership development is a $366 billion industry: Here's why most programs don't work." Forbes, June 20, 2019.

12. **Can you do something about it? A study of over 3,000 leaders . . .** Folkman, Joe, Personal communication, February 24, 2022.This is from the Zenger-Folkman 360 survey data set of leaders who had a pre- and post-leadership training program assessment. The analysis was conducted in 2016. Leaders from nearly 100 organizations/units were involved and the time period between the pre- and post-assessment ranged from 18 to 24 months.

Chapter Three:

1. **The popularity of Carol Dweck's mindset. . .** Dweck, Carol S. *Mindset: The New Psychology of Success.* New York: Random House, 2006.

2. **And Brené Brown's courage and vulnerability. . .** Brown, Brené. *Dare to Lead: Brave Work. Tough Conversations.* Whole Hearts. New York: Random House, 2018.

3. **Microsoft now tells its leaders. . .** Hempel, Jessi. "Satya Nadella on growth mindsets: The Learn-It-All Does Better Than The Know-It-All." LinkedIn Blog. *Hello Monday,* December 9, 2019. www.linkedin.com/pulse/satya-na-della-growth-mindsets-learn-it-all-does-better-jessi-hempel-1e/

4. **Even Amazon updated its original fourteen values. . .** (accessed 2021, July 16). AWS Culture, Leadership Principles, https://aws.amazon.com/careers/culture/

5. **Let me be clear as we start off, not all leaders are coachable. . .** Kellett, T. Director of Coaching Network Hogan Assessment Systems, personal communication, July 21, 2020.

6. **Academic research confirms the detrimental effect . . .** Ashford, Susan J. and Northcraft, Gregory B. (1992). "Conveying more (or less) than we realize: The role of impression-management in feedback-seeking." *Organization Behavior and Human Decision Processes,* vol. 53, no. 3, 310–334.

7. **Is coachability just a trait. . .** The findings for this section stem from my ongoing research on coachability. An initial set of 188 leaders comprise the personality analysis, with positive correlations based on the Hogan Leader Focus personality assessment, Zenger-Folkman Extraordinary Leader 360

survey and my Coachability Practices Review (CPR) assessment. The work is ongoing as I continue to add leaders to the analysis. Please note that many of the academic journal articles referenced in this book also contributed to the traits that help/hinder section.

Chapter Four:

1. **The U.S. Army's Center for Army Lessons Learned...** Darling, Marilyn J. and Parry, Charles S. "After-Action Reviews: Linking Reflection and Planning in a Learning Practice." Marilyn J. Darling and Charles S. Parry, REFLECTIONS: *The Sol Journal*, vol. 3, no. 2 (December 1, 2001).

2. **Research reminds us that we tend to limit our feedback-seeking efforts...** Froehlich, DominikE., Beausaert, Simon., and Segers, Mien. "Similarity-Attraction Theory and Feedback-Seeking Behavior at Work: How Do They Impact Employability?" *Studia Paedegogjica*, vol. 6. no. 2 (2021)

3. **Steve Moss, president of Executive Springboard...** Moss, S. personal communication, May 6, 2021.

4. **Executive coach Marty Seldman...** Brandon, Rick. and Seldman, Marty. *Survival of the Savvy: High-Integrity Political Tactics for Career and Company Success*. New York: Free Press, 2005

Chapter Five:

1. **Dailey & Associates...** Dailey & Associates. (2010, December 1) "Santa Sessions." www.youtube.com/watch?v=2j1FlcM9EeQ

2. **As authors Douglas Stone and Sheila Heen admit in their book...** Stone, Douglas. & Heen, Sheila. *Thanks for the Feedback: The Science and Art of Receiving Feedback Well*. New York: Penguin Books, 2015.

3. **Researchers have found that establishing a routine helps quiet the negative emotions receiving feedback...** Nasso, Selene., Vanderhasselt, Marie-Anne, Schettino, Antonio, and De Raedt, Rudi. "The Role of Cognitive Reappraisal and Expectations in Dealing with Social Feedback." *Emotion*. Advance online publication. (September 2020), http://dx.doi.org/10.1037/emo00008

4. **Scott later passed along an adaption of the description of actor noting taking...** UMW Theater. "Actor's Etiquette." January 2017. https://cas.umw.edu/theatre/files/2014/04/Actors-Etiquette.pdf

5. **They recognize that the gift of feedback is often messy and poorly wrapped...** Credit for the poorly wrapped analogy goes to the delightful book, *Where's the Gift?* Bristow, Nigel. and Bristow, Michael-John. *Where's the Gift?* Using Feedback to Work Smarter, Learn Faster, and Avoid Disaster. Utah: LCI Press, 2015.

Chapter Six:

1. **Researchers have found that receiving feedback without reflection...** Alvero, Alicia M., Bucklin, BarbaraR., and Austin, John . "An Objective Review

of the Effectiveness and Essential Characteristics of Performance Feedback in Organizational Settings (1985–1998)." *Journal of Organizational Behavior Management,* vol. 21, no. 1 (October 2001): 3–29. doi.org/10.1300/j075v21n01_02

2. **Having a simple process to guide us can be invaluable.** . . Anseel, Frederik, Lievens, Filip, and Schollaert, Eveline. "Reflection as a strategy to enhance task performance after feedback." *Organizational Behavior and Human Decision Processes,* vol 110, no. 1 (September 2009): 23–35. doi.org/10.1016/j.obhdp.2009.05.003

3. **The use of checklists to aid performance.** . . Gawande, Atul. *The checklist manifesto: How to get things right.* New York: Penguin Random House, 2014.

4. **As Saul Alinsky pointed out.** . . Alinsky, Saul.D. *Rules for radicals: A practical primer for realistic radicals.* New York: Vintage Books, 1989.

5. **Chris Argyis, the late Harvard Business School professor and author.** . . Argyis, Chris. "Teaching Smart People How to Learn." *Strategic Learning in a Knowledge Economy,* (2000): 279–295. doi.org/10.1016/b978-0-7506-7223-8.50015-0

6. **Research points to the value of adopting such a habit** . . . Lanaj, Flodiana, Foulk, Trevor, Erez, Amir, and Chen, Gilad. "Energizing Leaders via Self-Reflection: A Within-Person Field Experiment." Journal of Applied Psychology, vol. 104, no. 1 (January 2019): 1–18.

7. **Nigel's three calendar appointments.** . . Paine, N. Personal communication, June 21, 2019.

8. **The ability to maintain perspective in the midst of action** . . . Heifetz, Ronald A. & Linsky, Marty. "A Survival Guide for Leaders." Harvard Business Review, vol. 80, no. 6 (June 2022):65–152.

Chapter Seven:

1. **I drew up a four-factor change formula** . . . Credit for insight from the work of Robert Kegan, especially Kegan, Robert and Lahey, Lisa L.. *Immunity to Change: How to Overcome It and Unlock Potential in Yourself and Your Organization.* New York: Harvard Business Press, 2009.

2. **Park downhill** . . . Glomb, Theresa. "Let's make work better." TEDxTalks, *TEDxUMN.* 18:35. www.youtube.com/watch?v=oCYeEt94EMc

3. **Recent psychology and behavioral economics research highlights the power of reminders and "nudges"** . . . Gill, Dee. "Replicating A Successful Nudge in Health Care: Advice for Skeptics." *UCLA Anderson Review.* (July 23, 2021). https://anderson-review.ucla.edu/replicating-a-successful-nudge-in-health-care-advice-for-skeptics/

4. **The current literature on habit-building advises starting** . . . Hill, A.V. *The Managing Me Workbook for Busy People.* Eden Prairie: ManagingMe.Solutions, 2021, www.managingme.solutions/workbooks.

5. **Executive coach Marshall Goldsmith uses a simple routine** . . . Goldsmith, Marshall., & Reiter, Mark. *Triggers: Creating Behavior That Lasts—Becoming the Person You Want to Be.* New York: Crown Business, Penguin Random House.

Acknowledgements

One author's name on the cover of a book can suggest a solo effort. In this book's case, nothing can be further from the truth. I'm grateful to many people who provided coaching, truth-telling, and encouragement along the way.

Thank you to those who helped draw out the idea of coachability in discussions and white-board sessions, particularly my mentors at the University of Minnesota Carlson School of Management: Dr. Beth Campell, Dr. Karen Donohue, Dr. Theresa Glomb, Dr. Stephen Glomb, Dr. Art Hill, and Dr. Mary Zellmer-Bruhn. Special thanks to research assistant Madison Schwartz for tracking down the volume of coachability research.

A special note of appreciation goes out to my Zenger-Folkman mentors and friends Dr. Jack Zenger and Dr. Joe Folkman for your generous help in diving deep into your Extraordinary Leader 360 database to provide the research underpinnings of coachability.

Thank you to those who took the risk to field-test the early concepts and tools of leadership coachability with their managers and clients, including Cathy Bergland, Mara Lawler, Christen Cole, and Kevin Copestick and Ryan Dunn. Like a skilled director, each of you provided Actor Notes after every performance to advance the quality and value for the next round of coachability training.

Thank you to my valued network of consultants, coaches, and

talent development practitioners who kindly donated their time to review rough draft after rough draft to bring the full story of coachability to life: Dave Aeilts, Ed Betof, Sarah Bridges, Michael Bungay Stanier, Leah Clark, Steve Cohen, David DeFilippo, Matt Donovan, Gerry Hudson-Martin, Pete Longhurst, Jim Louwsma, Kevin Martin, Mark McCloskey, Kjirsten Mickesh, Stephen Moss, Kevin Oakes, Jeff Prouty, John Russett, Dan Schulzetenberg, Joshua Seldman, Steven Snyder, Kathleen Stinnett, Jean Storlie, John Sweeney, Nick Tasler, Brad Taylor, Diana Thomas, Mark Urdahl, Scott Weisberg, and JW Womack.

Thank you to my work colleagues, coaching clients, and graduate leadership course students over the years who taught me much more than I offered them. Many of you may find something familiar in reading the case studies in this book. While all of the names and some of the circumstances have been altered for anonymity, I do have to call out a few specific names of mentors and career friends, starting with Dennis Mannering and Jack Schleisman, who sparked my lifelong fascination with leadership development back in my high school days, and later to those in my "general" days, including Dick Roedel, Steve Kerr, and Steve Mercer in my GE days and Mike Peel, Mike Davis, Jacqueline Williams-Roll, Ricardo Aparicio, Beth Gunderson, Joe Mucha, Michele Emerson, and Omar Douglas during my General Mills days. Also, a note of thanks to my original side-gig leadership consulting partners Scott Cabot and Ron Wallace.

Thank you to those helping through the writing and publishing journey, starting with Sara Jensen, writing coach extraordinaire, and my publisher Beaver's Pond Press, and their constellation of experts guiding the book creation process, with special appreciation to Tina Brackins, Courtney King Bain, and Becca Hart.

A final deserving note of appreciation to my family: To my loving and forgiving wife, Mary, thank you for gently reminding me to keep practicing what I teach about coachability; to my daughter,

Sarah, who found out early that Dad has good ideas but let Mom double-check her school writing assignments; Finally to my parents, Don and Pat Wilde, who kept taking their third-grader day after day to a Carnegie Library in Hartford, Wisconsin to spark a love of reading. It worked.

About the Author

Kevin D. Wilde currently serves as an Executive Leadership Fellow at the Carlson School of Management, University of Minnesota. He teaches applied leadership in several graduate courses. His current research topics include leadership coachability, executive derailment, and contemporary talent development. In 2015, he concluded a thirty-four-year corporate career in leadership and talent development at General Electric and General Mills.

During his time at General Mills, the organization was consistently recognized for its innovative development work, highlighted by *Fortune's* #2 ranking as one of the best companies in the world at leadership development, #1 listing by Leadership Excellence magazine, #1 Global Learning Elite ranking, and *Training* magazine's "Hall of Fame" designation as a top company for employee development. In 2007, *Chief Learning Officer* magazine selected Kevin as CLO of the year.

Kevin continues to be an active contributor to the leadership and talent development profession with business advising and writing. His advisory work includes the Institute for Corporate Productivity (i4cp), Study.com, and GP Strategies/Learning Technologies Group. In 2011, his first book, *Dancing with the Talent Stars: 25 Moves that Matter Now*, was published by Human Capital Media. In 2015, he served as editor of *A CLO Leadership Reader: Chief Learn-*

ing Officer Magazine's Best for Today's Learning Leader. His writing for *Talent Management* magazine received a national award for editorial excellence from the American Society of Business Publication Editors. His work has also been published in over a dozen books, including *Coaching for Leadership,* the *Pfieffer Annual on Leadership Development,* and *Forward Focused Learning.* While actively researching, writing, and teaching, he first and foremost considers himself a student of the game of leadership and believes there is always something new to learn.

Made in United States
North Haven, CT
01 September 2023

41014328R00098